When Everything Ain't Copasetic

A lot of things happen that I don't really understand but at my age I've grown pretty content in reciting the serenity prayer and calling it a day. There are a lot of things that I simply don't understand but being that my whole being and longevity revolves around becoming at peace with myself and with the world in which I reside. I am not overly concerned with too much aside from the basic necessities of life and my writing.

However, because I don't go out in search of doesn't mean that these things, (nuisances I call them), don't see fit to try to intrude on my meager existence. It's almost as if my peace is somehow unsettling and unnerving to them. And so out of compulsion they intrude.

There was a time when I was rather accommodating to their needs but as I grow older I see their worth declining in the whole scheme of things for me and that's not to sound harsh or chauvinistic or mean that I am becoming more of an egotist than chauvinistic but I find little or no place for women in my life at this juncture.

I've given this considerable thought over the last year or so so contrary to my very nature it is but I have come to the conclusion that in the whole scheme of things I see and have no place for them at current. Now that is not to say that I prefer males any better as a whole but I can at least stomach them for short periods of time without becoming nauseated whereas women I've long since grown short with.

When examining the reasons for this latest phenomenon I have to say honestly that I have over the years entrenched myself with attaining logic in an all but illogical world. That is I have both consistently and conscientiously tried to sit back and make sense of the cosmos and in so doing so understand where I fit in in the grand scheme of things.

This is a meticulous and painstakingly endeavor with miniscule gains at most. But over a lifetime of acquiring knowledge and classifying it in its proper nomenclature to where it makes sense to me I have a hard time with those that do their best to enter my world of organized thought with mindless ramblings on inconsequential subjects that just come to mind such as:

"Bay, do you think I'm losing weight. Everybody at works says how I've lost weight," to which I reply, "Sweetie pie, I married you when you looked like Free Willy. So, do you think I'm really

Memoirs of a Delusional Diva
The Jewel That Was No Gem

By

Bertrand Brown

concerned with your weight?" To which she replies, "But Bay I just want to look good for you at your family reunion."

Mindless ramblings when the family reunion is tomorrow so if you haven't done it now I don't think there's really any need to have this conversation." It's at this time that she puts another Chip-A-Hoy in her mouth.That's only one small example of a gender whose thought pattern is a hodge-podge of mindless ramblings and I am so convinced that we, (not Eve), are to be punished for the original sin.

Here's another example of the mindless banter that keeps me confused and my mind in a quandary and keeps me babbling the Serenity Prayer as though it is the very lifeblood that keeps me from drowning in a sea of chaos.

A man was riding by our home one day about six thirty one cloudy and rainy morning when a piece of the roof flew off of the house and hit his truck. Being that he was a roofer he stopped and rang the doorbell and told me the story of the shingle and the truck. I was glad that he didn't seem too upset but and since he wasn't I wondered why he had stopped at all. That's when he shared me with the knowledge that we needed a new roof. This however wasn't exactly new news to me as any time it rained the walkway up to the house was always strewn with shingles and debris from the roof. What he did however was give me his card and share the fact that whenever we decided to do the roof we should keep him in mind.

The roof, however was not of supreme importance at this point however as I continually wondered when I would hit that soft spot on the kitchen floor and wind up in the basement. The linoleum gone by this time and the wood showing through I wondered how long it would before we would all end up in the basement. Still, I refused to lend a hand in replacing the floor as Jewel was content to give any extra money she had to the newly built Rivers Casino.

But the roof and the kitchen floor were not our only problems. We had a garage door which was not functioning. One window was broken out giving easy access to the entire house which didn't pose any immediate threat to my wife who possessed nothing of value and should it have been broken into or better yet burglarized the thieves would have been very disappointed and probably donated something on behalf of the house.

I really wish I could say that that was the end of the maintenance problems but right at that time the toilet stopped working. Now and although I didn't have the money I called Roter Rooter and his cousin Mr. Rooter to come and look and give us an estimate on fixing the toilet. I believe one quoted us twenty eight hundred and the other thirty-six hundred. But my mother-in-law and dear wife who watches just a bit too much HGTV decided that they were both trying to rip us off and didn't know what they were talking about although they are plumbers by trade Jewel decided to fix it herself. Now on that note I must digress a bit. My wife likes challenges and projects and installed the toilet herself and I must say it's a fine toilet but not your standard height. And although I am short I have never in my life been to anyone's house where I need a stepstool to get on the toilet. Once seated I have to hold onto the toilet seat so as not to lose my balance as my feet come nowhere near the floor.

She also did the tile in the bathroom which stops a few feet from the tub. I was curious to whether she was trying to devise a moat to circle the tub as she has this preoccupation with Medieval Times.In any case, those are a few of the problems with this house she seems to love so much but those are not the only ones. All of the doors are either worn out or malfunction in some way. But there is one in particular that riles me to no end. You see I've designed a portion of the house to satisfy my needs that being the basement. Here I have a converted bathroom which she was planning to turn into a spare bedroom. This is my clothing closet and outside of that is a large room which serves me as an efficiency apartment with two sofas, a large desk, a big screen TV with no cable that acts as my entertainment center as I also play my music, (but not too loudly), and my desktop computer. At the top of the stairs is a door which like most of the doors does not function. On several occasions I have closed it or she has closed it and I have spent hours jiggling it and talking to it to get it to open. On one particular night I fell asleep downstairs and was hard pressed to get back upstairs to go to bed. I must have spent two hours trying to open it as I do not sleep down there as it used to be home to a rat the size of Godzilla. But after two hours of jiggling, and praying and talking to this door I gave up and had to go outside through the garage, (that's the door that cannot be locked), to go upstairs and knock on the front door to gain admittance. And with all of these problems at hand she asked me would I rather go to Ocean City or Virginia Beach. Sometimes I question her sanity. With all of the immediate problems which ail us I wonder how she could think of taking a trip anywhere.

The Toilet

As if that isn't enough the toilet was stopped up and the basement had an inch of water on the floor. At first I wondered if she were building an indoor pool. But after the mushrooms started growing from the carpet I thought that perhaps we were just encountering another problem associated with having an older home. Still, it was all a bit too much for one who has lived in everything from a small mansion to my last two homes which were built from the ground up. In any case, she confessed that these plumbing problems were annual ones and that she knew that the basement flooding and the toilet malfunctioning were not connected. The plumbers thought they were but alas my wife who has never been to school for plumbing disagreed and because I have learned that to argue with her could result in temporary homelessness I agreed. I did share with her the rather universal idea that the cost of owning an older home could be astronomical and cautiously suggested we downsize and move.

Now as I told you before she is quite adamant about almost everything and after having called the real estate broker in and painting much of the upstairs she said she had security in this home and wasn't moving anywhere. Partners from the time we said I do I saw that my opinion hardly counted and so we spent my second summer watching the toilet fill up with shit and then scooping it out by hand and walking buckets of do do to the tree line in the backyard and dumping it. As I said this went on for the entire summer until I could take no more and was thrown out or sent to jail for talking shit, (I can't remember now), for my monthly respite.

I returned, (out of stupidity or love—which I believe now are synonymous), and a month or so later the house was broken into by some of her family members. Well, in actuality they didn't break in. They simply came through the garage door and stole both laptops and a jar of change. And still I stayed.

Work and Financial Management

Before I arrived in Pittsburgh with this woman I weighed somewhere around two hundred pounds and being I am only around five foot two I must admit I was overweight.

At the time I resided in Greensboro, North Carolina. Now Greensboro is a college town with no less than six colleges and is predominantly Black with many of its inhabitants from New York City. In recent years there has been an influx of Africans. And being that I am from New York and of African descent I was right at home. In fact, I loved it. I loved the fact that it was cosmopolitan in a sense and yet moved at a moderate pace.

In any case, I was happy there. I'd just written my first novel that did fairly well and I worked a couple of days a week at the local flea market and did as well if not better than those working a seven day forty work week. I'd spend the majority of my days at home on the living room sofa watching the latest movies and listening to the latest music. I guess you could say I was music and movie critic as I sold bootleg music and movies. And since I'd been doing rather successfully for the past fifteen or sixteen years I'd become pretty proficient at it. I had to be. With a mortgage that fluctuated between twelve and fifteen hundred dollars a month I had to be on the grind twenty four seven. Still, that's not all I sold. I sold African art, books, women's clothing, brass, and anything else I could get my hands on that my constituents seemed to have an inkling for. And when I got finished selling I'd retreat to the comforts of my home and get ready for the next week. There was no such thing as vacation days or paid holidays but there was certainly plenty of overtime.

There were times when all I wanted to do was let go and run and hide. My phone rang incessantly and people were constantly stopping by either to get an item early or to show me something new with the hopes of selling to me. I had no credit cards and there were no credit checks with the people I dealt with. I had a reputation and if I saw something I wanted I took it with my word as my promissory note that I would pay them when I said I would. And this is how we did business and I loved every minute, second and hour of hustling. On a good week it was not uncommon to bring home twelve or thirteen hundred and on a slow week I might make as little as six hundred and would curse myself because I knew I hadn't pushed myself to the limit.

My best friend and major competition was an African named Max who would call me every day. When he'd call I knew it was neither to go golfing nor to have a drink but time to hit the streets. And hit the streets we did. Not to be in competition I'd usually go to help him sell his wares and well just because I loved making the sale. The only time I did go sell during the week is if there was something that caught my eye and I just couldn't do without, (which happened a lot). But I was no stranger to work and did my best to instill this in my children.

Now I have had the opportunity to live in a number of places and regardless of what my profession was at the time I'd learned two things concerning work. The first was that work wasn't nothin' but a job. And the second was that a J-O-B meant nothing more than being just over broke so wherever I lived I hustled and I hustled hard. I've always lived well which to me means having the everyday things—you know—the basics. But living well was never quite enough for me and mine. I was brought up spoiled and having the best of everything. And I couldn't see abandoning this for a common everyday existence which meant just getting by. When I ate I wanted lobster and prime rib. When I drank I wanted top shelf, (although I went through a stage where Keiths Wild Irish Rose was my drink of choice). Clothes, I had to have the newest and latest of everything. And when my children came into the world they encountered the very same lifestyle. Of course, it meant me cutting back on some of my own luxuries but I made sure that as long as they did well in school they could ask for anything they wanted.

Aside from that I enrolled my daughter in ballet and dance and kept my son active in sports and martial arts. Along with that I made sure that they had flute and clarinet lessons. I never wanted them to have any distractions in school and never to think sneakers and other articles of clothing were anything but clothing so I bought them whatever was popular making clothes commonplace rather than special.

There was one key ingredient however. They had to put in the effort and hustle just as hard as their father did and with hard work the world could be yours. At least that's what I stressed to them and I am extremely happy to say that at nineteen and twenty-five they have embraced the concept and have not only completed college but have a great work ethic.

Sometimes I digress when it comes to my children who I love dearly. But in going back to hustling and persevering I'd like to recall a couple of small anecdotes and then relate them to my current situation.

My parent's retired from working and headed to Fayetteville, N.C. in their twilight years and being that my mother was a stay at home mom and raised my sister and I while my father was Chairman of the English Department at City University of New York when he arrived in Fayetteville he bought my mother a restaurant in appreciation of her being a fine mother and wife.

A graduate of the Helen Worth Cooking School, was one of her many accolades; a college graduate, painter, author, gourmet cook, newspaper columnist, teacher just to name a few. But first and foremost she was industrious and perhaps the hardest worker I know; cooking for a hundred or so loyal customers a day. In any case, grateful for all that they'd bestowed on me I moved south to help them with the restaurant and became their dishwasher and delivery person. I taught middle school in the daytime before leaving for the restaurant where I worked until seven or eight at night, washing dishes. And I wrote the sports column for the local newspaper when I went home at night.

During my breaks at the restaurant, (which were frequent), I would stop at the baseball card and memorabilia shop two doors down from the restaurant. Knowing little about cards I listened and learned and began collecting until it not only became my hobby but my passion and my fetish. I soon had closets and any spare area filled with boxes of cards and like shares of stock I sat idly by waiting for them to rise in price and many of them did. I bought some boxes of Leaf baseball cards, (that was the brand name), for forty dollars a box and watched them go to a hundred and twenty dollars a box in a matter of weeks and decided that it was time to open my own shop. Along with my friend and financial backer Sheila Hopkins I found a small booth in the back of a flea market and opened shortly thereafter. The first weekend we made a little over fifteen hundred and I was hooked. I can still here my mother saying don't quit your day job and I guess she was the only reason I continued teaching for as long as I did. I absolutely loved it. I loved the selling aspect, the social interaction, the gambling on prospects. I loved everything about it. A couple of years later the business became swamped with overzealous card makers who starting producing tons and tons of cards and oversaturated the market. And by then I was making between eight hundred and twelve hundred a weekend. I bought a BMW and as my wife and I weren't exactly getting along and since money attracts the young and the beautiful I moved around the corner from her and sublet a townhouse in the same complex.

When the card business died I moved to Charleston, South Carolina and found a full time and part time job as an instructor with the state. Having my son with me I knew I had to pick up the pace to afford him with all that he did not need and so with two jobs I again began hustling on the side. I said all that to say that if one has needs and desires as I do then working along will not afford you the creature comforts and little extras that you may want so in turn you must strive for that added extra.

Which brings me to where I am now. As I've stated previously I married Jewel, a woman who I think I'm madly in love with. (Well, that is on the good days. There are other days when I am forced to ask myself what kind of fool am I?) In any case, she is both quite controlling and jealous to a fault. I believe I stated that she claims drinking is the route of all of our problems and although I have stopped drinking we continue to have the same problems. Most of our problems reside in her inability to manage money and having little or no discipline and as well she may like this kind of life I need order in mine.

One year ago at Christmas time, I put the down payment on a car that she wanted as a Christmas gift. Six months later after assuring me she could make the payments the car was repossessed. It now sits in her mother's garage because she cannot pay the taxes, insurance, etc. to keep it on the road. That same Christmas I bought her the top of the line phone which cost me somewhere in the neighborhood of two hundred and fifty dollars. The phone has been off more than it's been on because she cannot afford to keep it on. I also bought her a forty-two inch TV and had to put a three hundred deposit on the cable because her credit is so bad. That deposit paid the first month's bill. We haven't had cable since the first month. (All this, of course is due to my drinking.)

Being that as it may, the two of us were lying in bed one night and I asked a simple question though I had to be careful how I phrased so as not to be behind bars again. I said, 'Jewel when people fall behind on their bills or are struggling to make ends meet what do they usually do?' Now before I tell you her answer I have to tell you that she graduated and went on to Duquesne where she graduated magna cum laude and received her master's degree. She said, 'I don't know. What do they do?'

'Get a second job or a hustle' I answered.

She looked at me incredulously. And it was then that I began to wonder again if I'd chosen correctly. Was she an idiot savant just a plain idiot. I'd spent a considerable time with her son and like so many others I realized he too was a bit slow and asked her if he were slow and if he had been tested as I had spent many years teaching Special Education she became inflamed and quite defensive and I attributed to his father who she admitted wasn't too bight but now I wondered if he hadn't taken after her as she had absolutely no common sense. (Years later, when he was in high school and it was basically too late she would call to tell me the school had come up with the same conclusion and wanted to test him.)

 To make matters even more concerning the bills were always in flux and it hardly mattered if I were working and bringing home a paycheck or not. One month the water would be off. The next month it would be the lights. It was all a bit too much but I hung in there. It was the first time I'd ever been through anything like this but being of the sort that believes when you make a commitment you hang in there I bit down hard and tried to keep a steady head but in reality I knew that at forty eight she was hardly ripe for new ideas or going to change.

When I questioned her about the local flea markets she pooh poohed the idea telling me it was too far to go and the like. Truth of the matter was Jewel wasn't about to have any husband of hers work in such an environment and I wondered when the lights would go off again. Now I'm not sure if her thinking concerns the prestigiousness of the job or not and I'm not sure if she's thinking about the risk factor. In fact I'm not even sure if she thinks anymore. And the reason I say this is because the day before the water bill was due to she told me that she was going out to flip the money. The only people I know that flip money are crack dealers and true hustlers and she was neither. In fact she is one of the most innocent naïve women that I know and that is one of the reasons I was so attracted to her from the outset but when she told me that she was going to flip the money I was dumbfounded. Maybe there was more than meets the eye and so I went about my business

as she left for the evening. A little concerned I held my breath.
She returned later that evening or should I say early the next
morning. I had to get up early and go to work so I was not apt
to get up at three in the morning to see if she had flipped it.
The next morning as I got up to take my shower and turned on
the faucet and it spit and hissed at me but no water came out I
just naturally assumed that she hadn't been too successful in
flipping it. But that brings us to another subject.

On an average week three or four overdrafts come in the mail
stating that she has spent too much and in the three years that
I've been here I've heard 'next month I'll be okay'. And three
years later neither she nor her finances are okay.

The Casino

I believe I mentioned before my long time addiction with drugs.
Now that I have been out of the life for several years I have a
fervent if not deep hatred for drugs and those who sell them.
But it's not just for drugs but addictions in general and to marry
someone with an addiction who is in denial is almost more than
I can stand.

Marriage in my estimation is based on trust and although I have
no fear of her cheating or cavorting I am nonetheless distrustful.
My distrust however, is not based on superficialities and
insecurities. My distrust is not even based on the fact that you
went to the casino to flip the water bill. That would hardly fall
into shall I say the category of a falsehood since I never asked
and you never bothered to say how you were going to flip the
water bill. At best it may be an admission but certainly not a lie
or a trust issue. The trust issue arose when you apologized for
messing up the water bill and swearing to God that you would
never do it again.

The following weekend, (the water was back on by this time),
Jewel got dressed up at one a clock on a Saturday which is a tell-
tale sign in itself since Pittsburgh has few if any places to
frequent and even less if you're middle-aged. Anyway, Jewel
who is always so tired from working all week and who more
often than not is content to sit in the living room in front of the
TV all weekend suddenly decides to start getting dressed on a

Saturday afternoon to go Christmas shopping with her seventy four year old mother and older sister. When I asked if I could tag along as I had some last minute shopping to do as well she politely said no because they were shopping for me and how could they shop for me with me there.

Anyway, she started dressing at somewhere around two and didn't leave the house until around nine which throws up alerts but then why would this throw up any red flags? The fact that I've been around a minute and a lot longer than Jewel means nothing when you have an inflated view of oneself.   But being an addict I know every conceivable scam and scheme known to man to get where you want to go. And so I listen and wait 'til Jewel leaves the house at somewhere around nine o'clock and call your mother—oh say—an hour later only for your sister to tell me that I know that mommy's always in bed by eight thirty. I then ask her if I can speak to Jewel since they are supposedly shopping together only for her to tell me that she hasn't seen my wife in two weeks. I thank her and hang up the phone.

I can now relax knowing that she won't be home until the wee hours of the morning and then with another lie so I lean back, turn up the music, and have a few drinks. It's now about one a.m. and I get up and walk down the block to Jewe's aunt's house. They're all alcoholics and so chances of them being up on a Saturday night are good to excellent and ask her aunt if she'd take me to the casino which is no more than five minutes away. I arrive hoping that my hunch is wrong and that I still have a marriage only to find my dear sweet wife, leg crossed, cigarette in one hand spinning the wheel. I never said a word choosing to just stare at this woman who I so loved and wondering why.

Ballroom Dancing

There have been other times but the one that stands out was a few weeks ago when Jewel told me that she and her friend Stephanie were going to Erie, Pennsylvania on a bus ride to go ball room dancing which was intriguing to me since there were two busloads going and in all of my fifty four years I have never known a Black man to go ballroom dancing—let alone a bus load. But that's what she told me.

I was at Macy's working when I got the call from Jewel informing me of her plans to go dancing. I was talking to a friend of mine at the time who happened to question the whole affair and it made me think. Seeing an older White woman in passing I asked her if she ever heard of people going to Erie to go ballroom dancing. Well, lo and behold the old White woman happened to be from Erie and she quite emphatically told me that there was nothing in Erie but gambling. I drove home, stopping by the liquor store and sadly wondered how I could have possibly gotten myself into such a mess at my age. I wondered how she could lie to her husband so easily.

I was for all intents and purposes retired and living the good life when this woman called. And now here I was stressed over money and what she would do next. I had a woman and a routine that was settled and a homebody who didn't run the streets anymore and who accepted my age and limitations and was content to build a home from the inside. But the woman I had chosen to be my wife chose to run the streets and stay out half the night and lie to her husband on a regular and consistent basis.

Anyway I resigned myself to getting out while I still had my sanity and so I went home and sipped and went to bed. About five o'clock in the morning the phone rang waking me from a deep sleep. I answered the phone only to hear the devil on the other end asking me to please come and get her from the bus. I knew arguing with her would only lead to me going back down to visit my old cell so I got dressed and rode to pick she and her girlfriend up. But being that they were one of the last to get off the bus I asked a middle aged Black man getting off if they went to Erie to go ballroom dancing—you know just to clarify things in my own mind. 'Nah, man we went to gamble,' he answered. Seeing her girlfriend Stephanie in her blue hospital scrubs I only wondered how many dances she danced.

New Year's Eve & Housecleaning

It's not enough that I am in a city that I dislike but there is also the fact that I married someone in a city I dislike with the hopes that she can make her fondness for it my own. I suppose that would depend on you first knowing your mate before marrying her which I would strongly recommend after this debacle.

In any case, it's my third year here in Pittsburgh and my second New Year's. This has always been a time I spent with family. But traditions change and my wife chose to be with her friends instead and so I did what I do in times of crisis. I found my spirit of choice for that particular evening and sat and sipped alone and lonely. Being that it's June I cannot recall the reason why we were separated on New Year's but I am sure it's something I did that angered her like asking her to cook or clean up the house or pick her dirty underwear up off the bathroom floor. Whatever the reason was for her leaving it did not sit well with me and me being outspoken since I was able to speak I'm quite sure I let her know that I didn't like the fact that she was abandoning me on New Year's Eve.

Of course, my wishes didn't amount to a hill of beans and so she departed. At the time I'd been married somewhere around two and a half years and was now almost sure that I'd made a mistake. We were from two different worlds and I can remember my cousin Michelle telling me one day I went up to Harlem to visit her that I wasn't settled. Never knew what settled meant at the time but have come to realize that settled meant mature and I strove to become both cool and settled. I began to enjoy each day and age gracefully and after having raised two fine children I knew that it was once again my time to relax and find the peace that had so long eluded me. And in this marriage I sought that. Yet, one can only be responsible for oneself and the woman I married somehow and at forty eight years of age was still seeking something and was hardly settled. And I could hardly understand her still wanting to rip and run. I'd done it for the past twenty years and could tell her there was no future in the streets but then who was I to say? After all, hadn't my parents tried telling me the same thing?

I thought the holidays were a time when family spent time together. That's what I thought but was I placing my values on others? I wasn't sure so when she was adamant about going out with her friends on New Year's I just naturally assumed she was going to her usual haunt. And assumed my natural role and had a couple of stiff one's and let the tears flow freely. I was broke, and she'd done her best to burn all my bridges, streets, lanes and highways that led anywhere. There was now nowhere for me to go and I felt like the words were tumbling down around me. The person I came here to be with had a life unbeknownst to me and I had nothing here; no friends, no job, no money, nothing. And she was leaving me on a night I was used to celebrating with family. My family had all but abandoned me because of my marriage and as I said she'd gotten rid of the majority of my friends. And now I was alone.

Before I continue however, let me tell you about a brief encounter I had with her mother the day after I proposed to her. Thinking it the appropriate thing I asked her mother if she had any objections to me marrying her daughter and was surprised when she answered quite unlike all the movies I'd seen.

'Are you sure that's what you want to do?' Once again I was dumbfounded or perhaps just dumb but I listened.

'You know Jewel's no housekeeper', which translated means my daughter's nasty. Still, I didn't hear her. 'And you know she doesn't cook.' She had my ear now. 'And you'd be taking on the responsibility of having three boys'. I heard her and was dumbfounded or like I said previously just dumb because I ignored what was a clear warning from someone who knew her much better than I could ever and still smiled. Are you sure that's what you want to do? At this point, in something like a drug related euphoria I answered with a resounding 'Yes'. I now know that with age comes wisdom but I chose to reject the old woman's wisdom and to jump off into the ocean knowing I couldn't tread water. Three years later her mother's words reverberate in my ears on an almost daily basis.

Maggots

Jewel and her son were less than clean and the house was always in shambles besides the fact that it was falling apart. It was disturbing but my speaking on the subject only angered her. She was defensive when it came to her house and reason hardly ever came into play.

One Saturday I awoke and walked into the kitchen as was my usual routine to fix a pot of coffee only to find that there was a trail of rice leading from the garbage bag, (I'd purchased a kitchen garbage can but they seemed to prefer the garbage bag on the floor and threw the garbage can out). Anyway the trail of rice led from the garbage can on the kitchen floor to the front door as if the rice were trying to make a great escape during the night to get away from all the dirt and filth. Seeing it she asked me what it was and so me not absolutely sure that it was rice running from the dirt and grime stepped on it with my bare feet to find that it was soft. She then informed me that they were maggots. Well, I had never seen maggots and didn't know anything about them other than they were nasty. But the maggots were nothing new. When I first arrived she gave me a grand tour of the house complete with its blood red dining room and multi-colored rooms. There was one room however with the door closed that she told me not to enter. At the time her two nephews and her son stayed in the room. Curious I opened the door and was at once sorry I had. The smell that hit me was atrocious and to say that it was a pigsty would have meant that some formal decorating had taken place. Clean and dirty clothes were piled on the floor and these served as beds for the three boys.

I exited as quickly as I entered and was glad to be out of there. I lay awake in the bed that night staring at her and wondered how she could possibly allow for this to take place under her very nose but take place it did and again I wondered if I knew this woman I'd chosen to be my wife. And so I raved and ranted and told them that they'd all have to leave if they didn't have that room cleaned up pronto which they did and from that day on they were assigned daily chores. For the most part and with rare exception they fell into line rather nicely—well all that is— except for my wife who just couldn't seem to wrap her magna cum laude brain around the fact that cleanliness is next to godliness.

And so two years later the house is still a mess and a disgrace most of the time and remains an embarrassment to me anytime anyone comes to step foot in the door. To tell you how bad it is, her mother has come by on occasion and asked for the broom and believe me her mother is no housekeeper herself. On another occasion her sister has come by and made the comment that she doesn't know why my wife doesn't keep house. On still another occasion my sister has come to visit me wearing a sheepskin coat and hat and refused to take off either coat or hat during her visit. I knew immediately what the problem was and tried to make her feel comfortable but I knew that the conditions didn't promote that. When my daughter came to spend some time with me she immediately asked me to go to the store where she promptly bought a can of Lysol and air freshener.

I was continually on my wife to be a better housekeeper but it wasn't in her nature and though she told me numerous times that she loved me she refused to show me or put forth the effort and accepted things as they were.

On top of that she wanted a dog. So now instead of just cleaning up behind she and her son there was another to clean up after. I refused and the dog peed and pooped anywhere he got the notion. After a while he found his spot and pooped in the same spot and after a while it got to the point where it had piled so high and gotten so hard that a visitor might have mistaken it for a piece of sculpture or a small coffee table.

I finally got tired of cleaning up after both of them and decided to seek advice on the subject and was told that if her gambling and filthiness are more stressful and unbearable than her love is then you only have one choice and that's too move out. It was a good point and I had to weigh it out carefully to come to a conclusion. In truth, I had no options since I was far away from home and had no money and knew of nowhere to go. Still, that wouldn't have been an option if she could have at least tried to adhere to my wishes as I had to hers. I haven't had a drink in over five months. Prior to that I was sober for six months because she requested I do so. But ask her to either cook, clean, or give up gambling and it's not possible. The effort isn't even there. So, I guess I have no choice other than to leave. You see if one is to put constraints on me that I give up my right to free will and abide their wishes because it makes them more comfortable and more at ease then I in turn should be able to get them to adhere to at least one of my wishes when it comes to something that really disturbs me.

I truly wish that these were all of the things that disturb me about this marriage but I'm afraid not. Funny thing though being a student of human nature I've come to realize that behavior can be modified if the right stimuli is introduced and so surely a parade of maggots or swarms of bugs in the kitchen where the food is would surely convince one to take a second look at the way in which they live.

Well, for most people that would be the case but not my wife. And so the conditions remained the same until I had firmly implanted the idea that it was her house and as soon as I was in a position to I would move out. Until then it was my sole objective to move downstairs where I could have not only peace but some order until that time. That was the plan. However, on New Year's Eve I watched as she went through the door, jumped in the car and drove away. Hurt and confused I drank myself to sleep. At eleven forty five I awoke to one of the stools at the kitchen counter being dragged across the kitchen floor and was just grateful that she had returned to celebrate New Year's with her husband. I called her name and when there was no answer I froze. Calling her several times and still no answer I looked around for a weapon but to no avail and so I looked at the port sized windows in the bedroom and considered jumping out. I'd lost considerable weight since coming to Pittsburgh because of her refusal to cook but I was still too large to fit through those windows. Panic was setting in and I had no idea of what to do or where to run. The front door was less than five feet away but as I mentioned earlier there is not a door in this house that works properly and I knew if I made a run for it I'd be murdered before I could manage to get it open and so I stayed put frozen and wondering what to do next. The suddenly it dawned on me that I had my phone. I thought of calling the police as we were pretty much on a first name basis by this point but reconsidered.

Then I phoned my wife and told her that someone or something was in the house. I was standing on the bed now a chair in my hand ready for anything that decided to come through the bedroom door. Standing there shaking and waiting for her to arrive I knew I'd called the right person. If anyone could have the police there in a matter of seconds she certainly could. But if there's one thing I can attest to—well besides her being able to summon the police in half a heartbeat it's the fact that she is never on time and I don't know how long I stood on that bed but it seemed like an eternity.

Standing there I reflected on the past week and the mysterious occurrences that had been taking place. One morning we got up and both the stove and microwave had been unplugged. She'd asked me if I was responsible and I just stared at her before answering. 'Yes, Jewel. I got up in the middle of the night because the stove and microwave had been on my mind and so I just unplugged them both so they wouldn't be on my mind anymore.' We were both puzzled and I blamed her sister who'd she's just put out and who hadn't seen fit to pay rent or contribute to the overall welfare of the household. But when both loaves of bread had been chewed open from the back I changed my mind. Now her sister is a big girl but even I seriously doubted that she would chew threw the plastic to get to the bread. No we had more serious problems. And after standing there holding the chair for a while my arms grew weary and I finally garnered the courage to make a break for the door. But first I yelled a blood curdling yell that probably woke up half of Pittsburgh and ran like hell to the front door which by the grace of God came open after only three tries. I was outside now and felt a lot more comfortable than I had been trapped in the bedroom.

A few minutes later I peeked around the corner and into the kitchen. The ten pound bag of potatoes that sat near the kitchen entrance had been dragged to the basement steps and I knew that it was not a two legged predator that I needed to be worried about but a four legged one. Still, what kind of animal could drag a ten pound bag of potatoes the length of the kitchen? It could only be a raccoon I thought. By this time my wife had arrived but refused to get out of the car. Some help I thought. After an hour or so I convinced her to come in and to this day she still hasn't said Happy New Year. She is a different breed of animal and I guess these things were never instilled in her as a child; just like the fact that it amazes me that she never says good morning in the morning or thanks the man upstairs for another day.

I cringe when I hear her wake up her son in the morning and negatives come out instead a positive word to prepare him for the challenges of a new day which is wrought with hatred and anger and all that accompanies being a Black boy in America. But anyway back to the animal which we now decided was living with us. I was convinced it was a raccoon and cringed at the thought that this unwanted guest was now living downstairs in the basement. I hated the thought of him of him decreasing the house in size and leaving me with no place to go. She had her room, her son had his room and well there was no room for me at all.

When we talked about our new tenant I was told that this was common to Pennsylvania households and I wondered if maggots, swarms of bugs in the kitchen, dipping poop out of the toilet, broken doors and flying shingles were all common to Pennsylvania households. I wondered if dirt and laziness were also common to Pennsylvania households.

In any case, I called Animal Control on Monday and two men came out and I was reassured that everything would be okay but they said that there were too many places for an animal to hide downstairs and would not put themselves in jeopardy by going down there and exposing themselves to an animal attack when there were just too many places for an animal to hide. Like the real estate broker who'd stopped by a few months before they suggested that the first thing that needed to be done if one wanted to avoid any more animals from making this their residence was to clean the house.

Funny thing was I understood. The only person who seemed to miss the point was my wife who was still trying to convince me that having rats was a common problem in Pennsylvania households. And that it had nothing to do with keeping a clean house. They left a cage which I checked every day and for two weeks it remained empty but it did not convince me that there wasn't something down there. After a month or so they called and said they were going to come pick up their trap which brought me back to the idea that there was something else also residing with us. They came and picked up their trap and being that a month or so had gone by I opted to hire two guys to come and clean both the garage and basement out.

I needed some space of my own and decided that I could design my own place and alleviate some of the stress of living in a way and a manner I was hardly used to. Growing up in New York and New Jersey, and residing in North Carolina and South Carolina where a nasty home was not the norm I decided to hire two high school boys and gave them a hundred dollars to clean the basement and garage. It took the better part of a week so you can imagine the state of things. On the last day they were finishing up and I was pleased at the way things were shaping up aside from the fact that they hadn't found the critter who'd taken up residence but there was evidence that he was living there as he'd eaten many of my clothes including the pants leg of a new suit I'd yet to wear. But on the last day they came running to the front door to tell me that in taking one of the sofas that was in the garage they saw the biggest rat they ever saw ran out from under one of the pillows. I didn't go outside to get a closer look but stood in the window and watched as they took baseball bats and chased him down the block.

Was there a lesson to be learned from not keeping the house clean? Well, let me see, there were maggots, and gnats and rats but alas there was no connection between these vermin and a clean house almost as if there was a synapse problem and there is no connection between vermin and a nasty home.

Discussions and Debates

Most people I know have spirited arguments. I deem a healthy discussion imperative to growth. There is nothing better than an exchange of ideas supported by credible facts to strengthen your argument. When I was in college I would frequent my friend Bea's apartment on a daily basis where there was always a lively and healthy debate on every topic under the sun. And I loved it. I mean I absolutely loved it.

Our moderator was such a friendly and cordial person that the house stayed packed with college students. Most of the time the topics would just arise out of the clear blue or an experience one of us had encountered with the predominantly white faculty. Race being so prominent most of our discussions revolved one or more of its aspects. Sometimes our debates or discussions would last for hours with people coming and going and adding their two cents. I excelled in this forum as I was well read and prided myself on my logic and liberalism.

To me there was never a clear distinction between the genders at this stage in my life and I believe this was in large part due to the forum I was in. The people that frequented my friend's dwelling place were often the best and brightest and there was little distinction between the men and women. Those that didn't share these qualities would shy away.

However, when I entered my current relationship appearances were often deceiving. It was easy to recite what had already been discussed but to ad lib and be a free thinker and use logic were often difficult. I was once told that intelligence does not in itself breed common sense and I often sit in total amazement at the lack thereof.

In Jewel's case the knowledge and the potential were there but absent was common sense or any sense at all for that matter. To me the worst thing in life is wasted potential. The very right to not acknowledge or exercise your right to be all you can be should be considered a cardinal sin. To not differentiate between emotion and potential is in itself a travesty.

Why do I say this you may ask? In the three years that I have resided in Pittsburgh I have changed my lifestyle though not willingly from a rather successful novelist who was retired and financially secure to a poor, wretch who neither knows whether there will be electricity from one day to the next or if he speaks whether he will be in jail or homeless. It's a difficult way in which to live and so each day I recite the Serenity Prayer and in the process of changing that which I can change.

A few days ago, my wife and I were walking to the bus and she asked me why I was walking in the street as opposed to walking next to her. My wife grew up here and is used to deer and turkeys taller than I am walking down the middle of the street whereas I am not. Funny thing is they have the right of way and will not move if they see you coming. The area we live in like most of Pittsburgh is fairly depressed and like most cities has a problem with drugs and crime. But being that she is somewhat naive she cuts through alleys and woods which she is at liberty to do as she is a woman, (at least in age).

Not I, however. In three years here I have had my brief case stolen, and the house broken into twice. I have had my wedding band stolen as well as my money stolen. Therefore I know that as hospitable and friendly as people may seem that it is still a city and has its elements.

Growing up in New York, you are given a survival handbook at birth which very descriptively outlines the do's and don'ts of the streets and everyone to a person is handed one at a day old. You grow up in survival mode. New Yorker's who have grown tired of the hustle and bustle of New York have migrated in large numbers to North Carolina and to a degree so has that element.

Let me recount two incidences where she was privy to this on her jaunts to come visit me. During the first account, she'd come down to visit one weekend and wanted to pick up an outfit to go out that night so I took her to Burlington Coat Factory which was chock full of Black folks. She found a few things including a pair of earrings. At the register while she was being rung up she decided to put the earrings on. Waiting at the door for her to finish her transaction we left and headed to the liquor store where I loaded up on my anti-nag medicine and put it on the counter only to find that she couldn't find her credit card. So busy had she been putting on her new earrings that she'd left her card on the counter when the clerk returned it and someone passing by had swiped it.

On the second occasion, there were two gas stations directly across the street from each other. One was frequented by the drug boys and other riff raff and the other by more normal people. I suggested that she being from out of town frequent the lesser of the two evils. But she not respecting a native's knowledge decided to go to the ghetto gas station and leave her windows down when she went inside. I got a call a few minutes later telling me that someone had stolen the cd's in the car.

Perhaps it's the six years difference in age; perhaps it's the fact that she has been sheltered all her life. (Her mommy still gives her a ride to work when she can't budget her money and takes care of her son when she can't feed him.) Perhaps it's the fact that she grew up in Pittsburgh. Whatever it is I don't know. I've heard that there are those called idiot savant that can play classical music as well if not better than the master's but could have a nervous breakdown if they be required to tie their shoe and sometimes I wonder.

Anyway, on this particular morning she's wondering why I wouldn't walk alongside of her as we traveled to the bus stop. The night before her fourteen year old came in the house a few minutes after his curfew, somewhere around ten fifteen with his thirteen year old cousin. None of them have any kind of common sense and leave fifteen minutes later to go to her mother's. Now I have two children and never would I have allowed them to come in past their curfew and then go back out and walk the streets at ten thirty at night but that's just me and the folks I know that value their children and realize what's out there in those streets. But I have long since and a few jail visits ago stopped interfering or giving my opinion on raising her son because of course she knows best.

In any case, I simply stated that I didn't put myself in harm's way and after three years of being around someone who never takes responsibility for anything that goes wrong I should have known to let it go at that point but I added that I don't put my children in harm's way and send them out walking at ten thirty at night. And why did I say that? She countered with, 'but mommy said' to which I replied. 'I don't care who said what I wouldn't have sent my fourteen year old out at ten thirty at night.'

Seems perfectly logical to me but she got to cursing and everything else so I promptly put on my headphones and picked up the pace until I was a good block ahead of her. When she caught up she cursed me out again for not wanting to walk with her.

When I initially got married she dragged me to Zale's jewelry store. I only had a week's pay on me; somewhere around four hundred dollars and as I stated before our home was wrought with problems. Most were of the nature that a good carpenter could fix. Then there were others that I tried to quell thinking that they were my own inadequacies and insecurities coming home to roost.

Aside from the fact that she'd previously been married was the fact that she and her husband had resided in this home. Being that this had been their home and she had a son as the result of this union I thought that moving would generate something fresh and new for both of us. It would give us a chance to downsize and have more money to do things such as travel and shop and well live. Anyway, she went in Zale's and purchased a ring for three hundred dollars and that was supposedly her wedding ring. Less than six months later she was again shopping for diamonds looking for a karat this time at close to two thousand dollars. It didn't matter that there was no kitchen floor, or that the car wasn't registered or inspected, or that we needed a garage door or that we would soon be looking up at the moon and the stars from inside the house if we didn't get a roof soon.

None of that mattered to her. And to tell you the truth I really didn't care except for the fact that I wasn't comfortable and hardly considered it mine even though I resided here. I wrote the whole damn thing off as it wasn't mine.

What bothered me though were the lies or better yet the untruths and I'm not so sure that it was the untruths but the fact that she wasn't bright enough to lie or outthink me. The bottom line was that she was from the country and anyway you look at it if you put a country boy in the big city they will eat him up.

In any case, I had questions, a multitude of them—you know to feel her out and to see where she was coming from and to get to know her. And every other question I asked her left me wondering. When it came to her ex-husband things were especially baffling. I asked her if she loved him to which she answered no but he made me laugh. So you married him and had a child with him because he mad you laugh. I won't go any further with that.

The full version of the story was hard to believe at best. And I tried. Seems that her father was dying and she was pregnant and because she wanted to do the right thing in her father's eyes she married him but there was no love there. Hmmm, that in itself is interesting to say the least. You can argue the point that you don't necessarily have to love a person to sleep with them. You can also argue the point that you don't necessarily have to love a person to marry them. I can relate to that and although I loved my first wife and still do 'til this day I wasn't in love with her by the time we got married but I had been living with her for close to fifteen or sixteen years so I questioned her sleeping with him and then marrying a person that she had never loved. I guess I wasn't supposed to have been that astute to have given it any more thought but then when her son was born she named him after his father. She then told me how she attempted to purchase him a barbershop and all this for a man that she didn't love r have feelings for. Picture someone naming their son after someone they didn't like and attempting to purchase a business for someone they don't care for and have no feelings for. I said nothing for at night she took care of my needs and if she wanted me to believe these things and kept fulfilling my needs who was I to say anything differently? Funny but she told me these things and I thought my God all I want is a start up on a flea market booth and you say you love me.

Perhaps I would be better off if I weren't loved so much because all I warrant is a jail cell and Mrs. Williams couch. For a man that she didn't love he certainly prospered.

She went on to tell me that the marriage only lasted a month and called me about ten years ago to tell me that she was emotionally divorced. I laughed as I had more women than I could deal with.

At the time there was Myrtle, Gale, Jackie and of course Cheryl. I drank then and must admit that all had nice homes, paid their bills on time and didn't have rats the size of large cats and I can't recall ever going to jail as a result of any of them. There was little or no drama and I was as always happy and tired and I politely told her that when she was legally divorced she might give me a call back since I don't do married women.

The inconsistencies in her stories threw up more alerts that the bitch was either crazy or a pathological liar. The jury's still out, (although I'm leaning towards her being crazy), but I never acknowledged or confronted her at the time. She also told me that although they resided together he stayed downstairs and she up and they never slept together. I bit my lip as I'd said the same thing to every woman I was interested in sleeping with on my way to their bedrooms.

Most recently I came across some movies, and with no cable I was glad to have run across them but being that I was in the bootleg movie profession for close to twenty years I have a pretty good idea when most of the movies came out. When I asked her if they were hers she told me yes but when I watched them and asked her if she'd seen each she said no which led me to believe that they weren't hers being that people who usually purchase movies know what movies they purchase and purchase them to watch them. But she didn't know any of her movies. Several days later I again asked her if they were her movies at which time she told me no.

Most of the movies were from 2004 and 2005 and unless he came over to drop the movies off as a token of his love for his family then he obviously overlooked them in his leaving. Funny thing is that a lot of the movies came out in 2005 which meant that he was still in the house nine years after they were married. But that's not the only thing. There were sneakers and clothes and though I've already said that she's not the most fastidious housekeeper what person has their ex's sneakers lying in the same spot in the middle of the laundry room in plain view after thirteen years?

What was even more interesting was that he was still receiving mail at this address up until long after I had moved in? You do the math. I've never been real good at math but to me things just didn't add up. But if that's what she wanted me to believe then believe I will. She kept me happy in bed and aside from that I could care less. Of course, he isn't here now but have her tell it it's because he loved women and the streets too much.

Knowing her now as I do, after four long years though I can see my epitaph reading something similar. He was an alcoholic and he abused me. It's all a bit humorous to me now as I ready myself to depart. I think of her ex and have to ask myself despite her saying that she didn't and never did love him. If he'd not chosen the streets and other women would she still be married to someone she didn't love? It would just seem to follow the pattern of I slept with him and I married him and I named my first born after someone I didn't love. Why not do twenty-five or fifty years?

Sounds absolutely ludicrous doesn't it?

I'll tell you this though after going down the same road I see nothing wrong with the streets or women after living this life for the last three years. My weekends consist of us getting up and her going into the living room and sitting in front of the television from nine in the morning until nine at night with no interaction between us whatsoever. Today she's mad because I stated that for reasons yet to be disclosed I would have to leave. She asked me not to speak to her and I agreed but I can't tell the difference between today and any other day.

When I was eighteen years of age I joined the Marines to get away from home and I can remember getting a calendar and crossing off the days as I got closer to finishing boot camp. I do the same thing now as I await my check that will allow me to get out of here and away from this woman. I tell her that I want peace and my impassioned cries are only met with her frivolous demands of what she wants never thinking of how this man really feels.

When you first meet a person you tend to look at them from a purely physical perspective but it takes years, for some a lifetime to come to get to know that person and the depths of their being. It is up to each one of us when we choose a mate to find out who that person truly is and to cater to their needs, wants and desires to become a part of their life and to get to know them better. I often do this through my writing as it gives that person another dimension and helps me to see them more clearly. I however am again wondering why it has taken me this long to see the obvious.

She told me she had a nervous breakdown when her father died and her marriage was on the rocks and after working in several mental institutions I would lay odds on the fact that there are some underlying mental issues prevalent here.

Education

My earliest remembrances of my father was that he was a teacher at Junior High School 52 in the Bronx. By the time I was eleven or twelve he was teaching at I.S.61 in Corona, Queens. My image of this is more vivid because I was older and his students used to marvel at the fact that I could walk into his classroom and answer any question he posed to his students. The reason for this was simple. I was around this genius of a man every chance I had as my father was my hero. Everyone loved him for his most gentle approach to life and education. A natural teacher he not only taught me everything he thought I should know but also used me as his guinea pig testing all his new curriculum and teaching methods on me his first born. I took standardized tests 'til they were coming out of my pores. And so when I was in third or fourth grade I had mastered the I.Q. Tests so prevalent then and was labeled just short of a genius and was maxing the standardized tests which only went as far as high school. At twelve I was reading on the twelfth grade level and was the pride of my parents.

In the summer I was giving a reading list long before schools had mandatory reading lists. I was encouraged to read everything from Alan Paton's Cry the Beloved Country to Jack London's Call of the Wild. And I never missed a word on a spelling bee from the first to the eighth grade.

They put me in the best parochial schools and by the time I got to school I was bored to death. I talked incessantly and was labeled loquacious by my mother who turned out to be my second grade teacher.

Both being college graduates and my father reached the pinnacle in education when after teaching English at Columbia University's Teacher's College he went on to receive his doctorate degree and later became Chairman of the English Department at Medgar Evers University in Brooklyn.   He went to co-author several books for the New York City school system. He also wrote a novel which the New York City school system turned into a basal reader. And on Saturday mornings when I'd wake up and turned on the television there he was moderating an educational journal.

Education was therefore a no-brainer for me and I knew as did most of my family members that college wasn't an option but a tradition that was to be followed. But like elementary and middle school; college bored me and so I finished in three years, (instead of the usual four), without attending classes on a regular basis. Most of my education was done in my spare time and at my leisure as I read voraciously.

I did my best to carry on the family tradition and am proud to say that my son must have gotten the message although I hardly thought he put forth the effort. When however he received a four year academic scholarship to the University of North Carolina I realized that my father's methods were still very much in effect.   Like my father I had a fair deal of success in the classroom and looking back have to say that was my calling. And like my father I took my son to sit in on my classes and he seeing my student's joy ultimately became a fan of his father as well.

That being said the climate for education is a mainstay and a priority in the Brown household and one that I am quite proud of. (My daughter is currently a junior at North Carolina Agricultural and Technical University.)

When I remarried for a second time to my current wife I was quite sure that my wife and I were on the same page . As I said previously she was first in her class at Duquesne. So, there was no need for me to question her commitment to education. Claiming to have taught high school I knew that she was committed to the task of educating as I was.

Now that I have become a part of the household I again wonder. Her son's school was across the street from the house for the first two years that I was here and she has yet to visit aside from his graduation. An avid reader she has and I can only speak for the time that I've been here not even put a minimal effort to infuse this into her child. There is little or no direction educationally and it is obvious in his grades and in his attitude towards education. Each day I ask him how school was and the pat answer he gives each day is the same. It's boring. And the reason I believe its boring is because he sees little or no value in it because it has not been fostered at home.

When I initially arrived in Pittsburgh I forced the boys to read and after a while the youngest read on his own and wanted to share what he read with you. He would be sparked by the newness of what he read the ideas overwhelming him and you could see the wheels turning and his thirst for more. Her son however was not sparked by anything and it was obvious that he had already adopted the idea that education wasn't cool and he'd much rather turn the other cheek, not put forth any effort in the cause of making himself the best he could be instead choosing to be average. It irked me to no end and made me hard to relate to him. There was no thirst for knowledge and I blamed his mother for not putting a significant emphasis on education.

It has always been my sole belief that if we give our children to the very same man that enslaved us why would we believe that this man has the best interest of our children and would educate them to be learned, intelligent and to compete with their own children. And after fifteen years or so teaching in school systems from New York City to south Carolina there is no way I would entrust someone to develop my child into the person that I would like for him to become. What would it profit to teach a Black male to have a sense of self and to take pride in himself and the accomplishments of his race? These things must take place in the home and are essential to a young boy to grow up and become a strong Black man.

But first and foremost it is our job as parents, as African American parents to teach when the school system has failed and to make sure that our children are in a position to make it in our absence and stand on their own two feet. Our job is not to coddle and baby our children but to make sure that we instill in them the discipline so that they are indeed independent when they come of age. Our job as African American parents is not to spoil them with iPhones and Playstations but to provide the skills so that they obtain these items when they come of age.

At times this is not an easy task and I'm willing to bet that no matter the time in our brief history as Americans has there been a generation of children that wouldn't have preferred to run the streets than to sit down and read a book. But we must recognize that we as parents are responsible for our children's growth and progression. We must realize that as parents we cannot simply say yes to all their whims. Instead we must pull back the reins and make sure that our children are inoculated and vaccinated against the disease of racism and capitalism that will have them incarcerated or on drugs or simply on the fringes of society and wondering what happened.

I have seen young Black men out their floundering trying to make it in a society they are in no ways equipped to make it in simply because their parents lacked the fortitude, resolve and knowledge to devise a simple plan to get their child from point A to point B. It is easy to dismiss those that suffer from generational ignorance but it is inexcusable when you have a mother with a master's degree that has a son who makes C's and D's in school.

As an educator it is easy to see the reasons for this. Perhaps there are many but those that stand out and are most evident from anyone observing from a bird's eye view. Being in the household I can see things much clearer than someone who can't see the forest for the trees. Being an educator I can recognize the problem. Being a parent I can feel her anguish. But the fact remains and even her son has said that he would rather his mother give him direction because with her lack of discipline and inconsistency he knows that what she says today will not be in place tomorrow.

She commenced to take me off the project and though she said she can handle hers he is slipping through the cracks little by little each day and will soon be lost. When asked about her son she is quick to say that 'he's a good boy'. I recently left jail and I am willing to bet that the mothers of everyone behind bars will attest to the fact that their son is a good boy including my own dear mother but the question is do you want a good boy behind bars or do you want a productive member of society with the knowledge and know how to thrive and survive in a society not meant for Black boys.

There has been long ongoing debate as to whether a Black woman can raise a Black male. And for a long time I refused to answer that question. It is an impossible feat but a possible one that many have had success with but after being in this house for a little more than three years I know emphatically that this is one cannot.

I try now not to watch although it is close to impossible not to see but I cannot stay and watch a young Black male like the ones I have fought so long and hard to save be emasculated and set up by a woman that has no idea how to raise a Black male. Whatever the reason she refuses to say no, provide discipline and give guidance and direct him to do the hard things which will help him in the long run is difficult for me to understand. Perhaps she does not know and this occurred to me but there are avenues to guide and resources to help her and with her being in the social services field and in charge of the guidance of young women how is it that she doesn't have a clue on how to direct her own?

There's obviously little or no support from the father when it comes to his son acquiring a good education then the boy is destined to be just like the rest of the lost children out there in those mean streets. So, and like so many of our Black males the sole responsibility falls on my wife. And when there is no communication between mother and father concerning the child's welfare, then there is no concerted effort, no plan.

It's like trying to travel to a place you've never been with no map. They're lost but not only lost because they do not seek help and utilize the resources right in front of them but because they are arrogant in their ignorance. And since we're on the subject let me ask you a rhetorical question? If you compliment on the fine job I've done with my son and you like the results then why not use the resources available to you or at least the patent and methods that enabled me to raise a strong Black man? In essence why go through the trial and error routine? Why attempt to remake the wheel when it's already been made instead of chancing error with your only son?

I have yet to figure it out but I can see the horrible, ugly end and this more than anything else will be the factor that removes me from this household. After all, I can stand the grief imposed on me but I cannot bear to watch a child being mishandled, misused and neglected because of sheer ignorance from someone who has used education to propel herself into the position she's in today.   June 22nd 2012

The Car

My dear father passed away a couple of years ago and left everything to his grandchildren. My sister and I being self-sufficient for the most part were not a concern and so he left us nothing. However, he overlooked an account and my sister called one evening to let me know that she and I were to split it being his next of kin. I was working as a caseworker with Allegheny County at the time and hated my job but had no thoughts of quitting or looking elsewhere. Most of the country was and is still feeling the aftermath of the Bush bash.

When I got the news I had visions of grandeur and only wondered if there would be ample enough parking space at the airport to park my Lear jet. And wondered how many Brinks trucks would pull up in front of the house and if the neighbors would be upset with them parking in front of their homes when they came to drop off my millions. I then thought of the frugal man my father had always been and remembered him me for cutting the lawn, going to get his Sunday papers, and doing my chores each week and how'd he give me a dollar and an I.O.U. promising to give me the other dollar the following week and realized that there was a good chance my sister and I would be splitting a grand total of about seventeen dollars at best.

I was shocked to find that he'd mistakenly left us about twenty two thousand dollars. We split the money and although I was still in a quandary when it came to this woman I figured that since fifty percent of marriages ended because of financial problems ours would survive in lieu of this blessing that had only been recently bestowed on us. Once again trying to be the good husband I had to put forth every effort to find out if I could save my marriage. Al I knew from past experience is that it hadn't been nearly this hard. In fact, it had been almost too easy. Cheryl didn't talk much, smiled a lot and was always grateful for anything. Down for anything, she loved to travel and if I mentioned a place she start getting our pennies together and before I knew it we were on a plane going somewhere. But I guess familiarity breeds contempt and though we seldom had problems if a good wind came by I could be swept away.

When the money finally emerged I was ready. It was Christmas and for the first time since I'd been in Pittsburgh I could do it the way I was used to doing it. The previous Christmas I'd taken her nephew to North Carolina with me for a month and he told me that my wife had given all three boys I.O.U. notes for Christmas. It was hard to believe that a woman who made in excess of forty thousand a year would give children an I.O.U. note for Christmas. I just shook my head. I was staying with my first wife and my daughter at the time and she immediately went to work on making their Christmas what she knew it should be. We'd always picked up second jobs to assure that our children's Christmas was like no others. And though she didn't speak on it she went to work to make theirs special even though she hardly knew them and blamed this woman for breaking up her happy household. (I'm sure she did it for me knowing how I felt about children and what Christmas meant to me.) Nevertheless, I had Christmas that year.

Now in a position for me to do Christmas the way I was used to I asked my wife what she wanted for Christmas. But before I tell you let me tell you this. Sometime earlier, my wife received close to eight thousand dollars from the government. Every day she would call me and ask me if her check had come. Each night she'd ask me how I was going to get my 'Mack' on or how was I going to spend my part when it came. I never responded because it has always been my belief that you don't start celebrating until you actually have said money in hand. So, I said nothing. When the check did come she asked me to bring it to her which I did. First we went to a check cashing place which wanted ten percent or eight hundred dollars to cash it. She exited the place saying 'they're crazy' and promptly headed to the bank which promptly took two thousand dollars to clear up her account.

Now at the time she had a huge monstrosity of a truck which was ten or twelve years old and had so many problems that it couldn't pass inspection. When she took it to the mechanic he gave her an estimate somewhere in the neighborhood of twelve hundred dollars. Her mother and I shook our heads and tried to make her understand that you don't put that much money into a car that old and with that many miles on it. But our words fell on deaf ears as she knows everything and so she had the car fixed. Not less than a week later she asked me what the green liquid was that was coming from under the car. I told her that it was transmission fluid. When she got in the car would not go into drive or reverse. She ended up selling it for two hundred dollars the same week she spent twelve hundred dollars on it. Oh yeah, she gave me a hundred dollars out of the eight thousand. I really got my 'Mack' on.

So, you can guess what she asked for that Christmas. She'd been searching for some time for a car although she couldn't scrape two pennies together and was over drafted every pay check. But I agreed and eventually she found a car in Ohio. And so one evening after work we drove up. I have no license and yet she expected me to drive back but again I acquiesced. Call him love which I now know is synonymous with stupidity but anyway we drove up only to find the car she wanted had problems. She settled on a Saturn Vue with no research done on the car. I gave her a couple of thousand said Merry Christmas went to the Applebee's next door while she signed the papers and threw a couple down. Finally, ready to go we got on the road. I had no idea of where I was so I had to follow her. I flashed her that I needed gas and we pulled into a gas station. There was a motel next door and I mentioned that I was tired and in no shape to drive and asked her to consider spending the night but she said no that her son was at home and needed to get back. And with that she left me somewhere I'd never been in Ohio and went home in here new car that I'd only just now purchased for her. I wasn't wondering now as I was out there driving and lost at 2 a.m. in the morning with no license that this woman—well –you finish the thought...

Where Am I Now?

I go to court the day after tomorrow. It's by no means the first time since I've arrived in Pittsburgh. Fact of the matter is that I've been to court more times in the past three years than I've been in the previous fifty years of my life. I've been drinking ever since I can remember. I believe I was thirteen when I used to steal a drink or two from my dad's bar. And I have dated hundreds of women and not a one has ever had the occasion to send me to jail until this one.

I am as I told you before very outspoken and passionate about my beliefs and after having spent so much time going straying to the left of my very birthright I finally got right and realized my potential and jumped in with both feet. So, I have no time and little patience for anyone off the beaten track. That's not to say that I'm not lenient and compassionate with those who were not nearly as fortunate as I was but I'm adamant that those within my inner circle that touch my life or that I allow to enter my life have it all together or at least are moving in that direction.

My wife who I assumed from the façade she proposed had it all together is perhaps the biggest disappointment thus far. She who holds her head high and appears to be so confident and so knowledgeable has no idea of the real world or what it takes to succeed. I guess what she lacks most is the drive and determination to combat the mundane and become part of the elite. When I say elite I am not solely talking money.

When I was growing up and what I taught my children was to strive for greatness. And should you fail to achieve greatness then you can be at home with excellence. But with the effort put forth all else will come handily.

 Whenever you go out don't dress down but dress up. How people see you is ultimately who you are. It's a self-fulfilling prophecy. Never do anything halfway but do it to the best of your ability and never compete against anyone but yourself. The standards you set for yourself should dwarf the others vying and jockeying for success. I've always followed this in everything I've done and am happy to say I've reaped the rewards on more than one occasion. With excellence money and all else will come. They are but minor rewards when you reach your ultimate goal. I know. I've had money. I've driven everything from BMW's to Mercedes. They were the by-product of drive, dedication, determination, hard work and faith in God.

When I wanted something I worked hard and when working hard wasn't enough I worked harder, oftentimes working not two but three jobs. If my parents had any fear it was that I was going to overdo it. But in my mind there was no such thing.

I can remember a brother a few years older than I who had the same mentality and perhaps it's a New York state of mind. We had both recently relocated to Fayetteville, N.C. from New York.

Anyway Acosta was from the islands originally and had worked his way to New York and now was joining me in Fayetteville. Anyway Acosta didn't have two nickels by the time he got there but told me one we were talking that if you were from New York and couldn't make it in N.C. something was wrong with you. We slapped each other five and fell out laughing. A couple of months later I was teaching middle school, working in the restaurant, running the local Black newspaper up to Laurinburg once a week to be printed, writing a sports column for the very same paper and working full time at a group home on the weekend. I had my sights set on a BMW and a townhouse. Six months later I had the BMW, the townhouse and had opened a business which was soon to be followed by another a few months later. Acosta took that same drive and determination and turned those same two nickels into a janitorial business that rapidly turned into a chain. Everyone who knows me knows that I am a firm believer in making the impossible possible.

Being that I've been dealing with drugs for far longer than I'd like to remember with their long and short scams and been a sales person for far longer than that it is easy for me to read and assess people in a very short time. So, if you don't come correct I will quickly dismiss you as life is too short. At my age I have more time behind me than I do in front of me so time to me is essential and there is little time to dally.

So when my wife called me for the first time in years and told me she'd read reviews of my book and always thought that she would be the first to write a book I laughed although I took her seriously. She was certainly bright enough.

When I tried to dissuade her from coming to N.C. she was adamant about coming and after saying no for two weeks she showed up and seemed quite glad to see me. Now there's no doubt about me being a nice guy and all but it has to make you wonder why someone would travel from Pittsburgh, Pennsylvania to Greensboro, North Carolina to see a man. Weren't there any men in Pittsburgh? I know if the tables were turned I wouldn't travel out-of-state to see her. I t had been at least ten years or more since I'd seen her and she really didn't look any worse for the wear. And after a couple of drinks we were talking as if it were only yesterday. She hadn't changed much. The woman I used to know had been carefree and reckless and the mere fact that she was in Greensboro, North Carolina with a married man showed that little had changed and somewhere after making love she asked me the chances for a relationship. Now those were some pretty lofty goals on her part. How pray tell did she expect to have a viable relationship with a married man six states away?

One drink had always been her limit and she almost seemed angry when she told me she wanted a relationship with no games. She frightened me a little and I had visions of Freddie Krueger and was afraid to say anything. Pouring herself another drink I watched as her eyes rolled back in her head and I held on tightly waiting to see what was going to come next. What came next and I suddenly realized that I didn't know this woman who sat on the bed across from me. This meek, gentle, little lamb I'd met when she was nineteen years old had turned into the Exorcist as she told me the rules of the relationship and how she didn't have time for any games. It was then that I came to the conclusion that whatever had happened in the ten or twelve years that I'd seen her last must have been traumatic if not devastating for this woman to Google her first boyfriend of thirty years ago and hunt him down and come to visit him knowing that he was married and hoping for something.

For me women were common place and I'd been the hotel route before. When it was over they usually moved on or called me back for an encore but most weren't interested in any more than the thrill of the moment and went on with their lives. But and though I've had women come to see me from out-of-state never did I have someone as forceful and demanding. Now if she gave her version she'd say she simply came to visit an old friend and whatever happened just happened and when she left we'd still be friends but that was not the impression I got when I looked into that demon's eyes. I was put on the spot and was scared almost wishing I'd never slept with her. So, when she made her demands I agreed.

She was in North Carolina every other weekend for the next year and sometimes every weekend. And I'd be lying if I said that I not only enjoyed her company and conversation but was enamored by almost everything about her and so I married her.

Funny, how things change. I was talking to a cab driver the other day about marriage and he was telling me how his wife so changed after they were married. He was a bass player in a local band when they met but after they were married he insisted on him quitting the band because she didn't want other women to come and see him. He's fifty six now and hasn't played in a band for close to thirty years even though it was his passion and his life he had to give it up because of his wife's insecurities. But when her insecurities manifested itself in other aspects of his life he had to let her go. Now he's fifty six and wishing he'd followed his dream and realized his potential.

I smiled listening and relating his story to myself and had to say that we shared a very similar path. Instead of me realizing my true potential now that my children are gone and I have a second chance at life I chose to let someone mold me and put me in a box that I don't fit in. My children are adults now and out of the household and I am pleased with their progress and it gives me another chance to realize and concentrate on some of the things that I couldn't necessarily give my attention to so steadfast was I in tending to their wants and needs as they were growing up. And now that the time has come for me to 'do me' I once again have constraints placed on me. There's no doubt that I am partly to blame for this but I just naturally assumed that a free spirit would allow another free spirit to move freely even within the rather constricting confines of marriage but I have never so controlling in my life.

I believe that every man controls his own destiny and should be allowed the freedom to choose the way in which he moves in and out of the sunlight of life which God provides for us. He alone has to meet his maker in the end and answer for his deeds. And whether he chooses to be Mother Theresa or the Mayflower Madam he should not be hindered in his movements by another man as he is the one that has to answer in the end.

Marriage, in my opinion is the union of two people. The marriage can and should be a supportive component where each should have the support and cooperation of the other to reach their personal goals and sit down to share the accolades of their successes.

But not here where the advice is constant and consistently negative. The advice can be understood and welcomed if succinct and sincere but when the partner has significant issues it would seem that they would concentrate on their own very blatant inadequacies before offering advice in trying to shape the other person's life.

I have met a lot of good brothers in my frequent visits to CH6 but lo and behold I am not so apt to follow their advice on how to proceed in life when they are in and out of the pokey. Similarly it is difficult to take the advice of a woman who has yet to go where I've been. Sloppy, unclean, with little or no parenting skills or financial acumen who has yet to at fifty years of age had a stable relationship... Please explain to me how she has the right to give advice?

The Book

'Oh my God! I can't believe you wrote a book. I always thought I would be the first one to write a book,' she screamed at me when she first called me six years ago.

I'd written a total of eleven or twelve since I received that call and had ideas for three or four more brewing. My first book had been published two or three years earlier and proved a modest success. I had spent ten years or more trying to find a publisher and another two or three years learning the book market. I'd read countless books on marketing and had watched my father do the same and so I was pretty well versed in the publishing business.

Jewel, an avid reader and a big fan of urban literature after having read more than her share finally decided that she could write as well as many of the urban fiction writers on the scene today and picked up the laptop one day and began her writing career.

Now you have to know my wife. This is a woman who can have an epiphany while being sucked up in the eye of the storm. One Saturday morning she woke up to find there was something wrong with the way one of the drapes was hanging in the bedroom. She jumped up, got dressed, and headed to Busy Beaver and bought a drill. When she got back I was still trying to sleep but all I heard was the sound of drilling for the next three hours. There were fourteen holes in one spot where she was trying to hang this curtain and when it was all done one side of the curtain hung while the other was just left hanging. I put the other side up and she put the drill under the bed never to be used again.

So, when she took on the arduous task of writing a book I took a deep breath and was surprised when she labored on day after day until she finally finished this monumental task. We argued and fought many a day during the writing of her book. If it wasn't over the content of the book then it was over the fact that she didn't cook or clean usually and now she did even less and left me with the three boys when she closed the bedroom door and went off into the land of fiction.

When she finished her first draft I think we both exhaled. As I attempted to guide her through the process I was again surprised at not only her ego but her arrogance. I relayed the message that my father had driven into me countless times when it came to writing. The art of good writing is rewriting. Now I am aware of the euphoria one gets upon the completion of a project but any good writer knows that that's just the first step in many. When I relayed the message to her I was told that she wasn't rewriting anything. I had to admit that she was a pretty fair writer and her first attempt was better than most and a lot better than some of the writers I'd attempted to read in the field of urban literature but had to question how much better it could have been with a rewrite or two. Still, there was no convincing her and I had long ago come to the conclusion that I had too much to do myself to concern myself with someone who was going to defy the very laws of nature.

For our second anniversary she was still trying to upgrade her ring and being that I was in no means able to shell out two thousand dollars to purchase her the ring and really saw no point in buying her a ring which she would lose as soon as the ooh's and ahh's quieted down. So, I talked to my advisors and they all suggested that I publish her book as it would give her a project and Lord knows she loved projects. She'd been shopping around for publishers, (not researching them but just looking at their websites). And finally coming up with Blackbooks, a publisher out of New York she sent them an initial payment of three hundred dollars she was unable to get the rest of the balance together. I believe that I mentioned that she was no financial genius and had a gambling problem. In any case, I decided that this would make the perfect anniversary gift and ignored her request. I trusted her judgment and had the book expedited so that it would arrive on her anniversary. When the book arrived she was never happier calling friends and family members and running out to the local bars, (I didn't think the local bar was the best forum to sell books but then this was the same genius that most homes in southwestern Pennsylvania had rats). In any case with no marketing plan she took every chance she could to sell copies of her book.

Again I told her that the writing was the easy part and I was happy for her. The hard part was selling the book nationally and the only way to do that without an agent, publicist, or major distributor was to sell it online which demanded time, diligence and an inordinate amount of patience. I know. I stayed up sometimes eighteen or nineteen hours a day marketing my first book but as my wife is lazier than most she chose to get a webpage and to market through a social networking site. Again I shook my head and wondered why she was so adamant in negating what those having so much more experience already knew.

My father used to always say 'why remake the wheel'. But there was no telling her and I sat back and waited while she chatted and marketed her book on Facebook each and every night. I watched while she had a webpage developed. I asked her, (as if I were speaking to a normal person), if no one knows you how in the hell or what would prompt them to go searching for your webpage. Is God going to send them an email informing the world that you have a webpage promoting your new book? What is going to make them visit your webpage?

I even took her to groups of webpages that were now defunct and again asked why and how if there's an oasis in the desert would a man dying of thirst with no clue and no map know where or how to find it. She ignored all of this. And so, frustrated once again I gave up.

The quarter ended a few weeks later and royalties were due with the condition that you must sell at least fifty books to receive a royalty check. She did not receive one and came to me more than a little angry that she hadn't received any royalties. 'Bay I sold more than fifty books didn't I?'

Now these are what my father used to refer to as optimum teaching moments and so I reiterated that selling books online is a painstakingly difficult and monotonous and although I didn't have all the answers I did do some research and received royalties continuously since my books debut. I even went so far as to purchase books on marketing your book for her. To this day she has not opened or read them.   But she did coalesce somewhat and asked me if I would market her books. (I guess I do know something after all.) So, I did so with all the gusto I did my own but being that she didn't research her publisher a year later she has yet to receive a royalty payment.

Court

I had a court date today. My wife was going to meet me there and have the charges of pulling her hair dropped. As I said before I've dated hundreds of women in my fifty years prior to marrying this woman and I have never ever been to court or jail because of a woman. Well, that is up until I married this woman and moved to Pittsburgh.

No heartthrob I have had my share of women who have hinted around the idea of marriage but I have avoided the idea of mariage like I've avoided venereal disease and white folks. And yet I fell victim to this woman who has caused me more grief and hardship than I have in my fifty years prior to marrying her.

Now she often compared herself to my former wife and of course I stroked her ego and told her how horrendous my ex was to keep the peace but in twenty five years with my ex never did she cause me the anxiety this woman has caused me in the past three years. We argue each and every week and sometimes I just stare at her in amazement. To say it was a mistake is a misnomer of the grandest kind. I do not believe the English language has a word that properly does justice to the error that I've made when I married her.

For three years I went against my very constitution. I had long ago said when I retired from teaching that I was never going to teach again. That did not mean that I wasn't going to teach children but also included women. If they weren't on the same level then they weren't for me but suddenly I realized that I had done just that. I had taken on the Herculean task of teaching a forty eight year old woman that her mother and first husband had already given up on and thrown in the towel. Never the quitter I endured even though I had long ago come to the conclusion that the help she needed was far beyond my teaching skills and methods.

If one grows up in the hood, (which I didn't), one learns survival. She on the other hand, grew up sheltered and couldn't make ends meet if she had a safety pin some crazy glue and nails to hold it together. She makes better than fifty thousand a year and doesn't own a towel or a wash cloth and can't keep food in the refrigerator, a car in the driveway, or a man. And though I consider myself an intelligent person I fell victim to her.

Obviously punishment for my philandering ways I have done my penance and am looking for the closest and nearest way out. Each night I pray for my social security check or my unemployment so I can get a room, any room, anywhere with the basic necessities which is much more than I currently have here. And those that know of my situation call and pray for me. I pray as well and wonder if I'm destined to die here in this living hell so bad is it.

To make matters worse I went to court today for pulling her hair when I should have choked her. Being that it was a charge of simple assault I should have at least gotten my money's worth. In any case, I go to court and she's sitting there alongside of me and of course I'm nervous.

The judicial system has a history of not being especially receptive to people of my persuasion and being a scholar I am well aware of this. In the cities where I've grown up Black folks don't do the police unless absolutely necessary. The only time you will see a Black person in contact with the man is if he is being apprehended. We have our own justice system but my wife sees me getting in a black jeep two doors up and swears it's with a white woman and decides to curse and call me all kind of vile names when I return that evening and in the end calls the police when I choose to ignore her. I saw no need to answer as I went out with my good friend Beatrice who I've seen a total of twice since college and her pastor friend Mark. I do believe that her jealousy took over and in talking to people I've come to realize two things. The first is that because she dated and took a married man from his wife and family that the idea that could happen to her is very real and paramount in her subconscious. I believe the other reason is that her ex cheated on her. Still, I have given her no reason to believe that of me so I see no need to explain. Yet, any woman that I happen to speak of whether she be co-worker or friend from the past turns her into somebody I don't recognize. At one point I was forbidden to talk to my ex-wife and daughter. Well, she didn't exactly forbid it but she made it clear that she didn't appreciate it.

On more than one occasion she called associates and told them not to call her husband anymore. I had a client when I was a caseworker with the county who used to call me from time-to-time to inquire about her case. I was absent from work for a

78

week and wound in the hospital due to my high blood pressure and the woman called to inquire about my welfare and she called the woman back from work, (unbeknownst to me), and told the woman not to call her husband anymore and from what the woman told me asked her if I was fucking her. At other times she's just called and asked them not to call her husband.

In any case, she became rather upset that I went out on this particular night and wouldn't tell her where I had been and being that I had been through this countless times before I turned off the light and went to sleep but she couldn't let it be so she turned on the light and each time I turned it off she'd turn it on til I simply broke the light. Still, she stood there taunting and provoking 'til I jumped up from the bed. Needless to say I spent the night in jail.

I went to jail and went to court today. Now she by no means takes any responsibility for me being in jail or court but agrees to drop the charges after the police tell her that she should go to court on my behalf since she has second thoughts about it.

However, at this time she's on top of the world because she's received her yearly bonus of a little more than three thousand dollars. (The refrigerator is still empty but that's another story). In any case, I meet her at court and my very supportive wife tells me that she's missing her meeting after informing her boss yesterday that she has to be in court today. In other words, 'you're on your own husband or I have more important things to do than to waste time being here to support my husband in court. That was the attitude in court where I sat wondering what my fate would be for three hours. Finally, given a chance to talk to the DA she walked backed spewing something about how I'd gotten her in trouble and left to go to Nathan's to eat before I was even called. That's love.

Night Terrors

It was an unusual day in the Brown household. There was no arguing, no fighting. It was one of those days I'd dreamed about and just come to realize when I was accosted and brought to Pittsburgh to begin my penance. It was peaceful. I went to bed and moments later found me fast asleep. Sleeping fitfully I felt her pulling me and screaming my name. I awoke with a start.

What the hell was it now?

"Are you smoking?'

"No," I answered puzzled and wondering how I could smoke in my sleep. But did not say anything.

"I smell smoke," she yelled.

Calmly I explained to her that no one was smoking.

"I smell smoke," she repeated.

I looked at her in an effort to discover what was wrong with this crazy woman now but could not come up with anything other than the obvious. She was nuts.

I tried to hold her, wrapping my arm around her and whispering that it was alright but she hardly heard me. In a trancelike state she jumped up and ran around to my side of the bed with the speed of light and did her best to pull the hundred pound oak headboard away from the wall.

"Do you see the smoke?"

I looked around the room but said nothing nor did I see anything resembling smoke. I watched as she continued to pull at the headboard.

That's when I moved towards the door. I didn't know whether she was possessed or what. There was no doubt that she was a few bricks short of a wagon full on a good day but this was too much and I watched as she struggled with that headboard and screamed about seeing smoke. I didn't know whether to run for help or to just get back in the bed and pretend that this wasn't happening.

I stood by that door debating the situation for a while and wondering what the hell was wrong with her but tired as I was I decided to just get back in the bed and ignore her. After all, she hadn't posed a threat to me and so I climbed back into bed with her still ranting and raving. It was at this point that I closed my eyes and prayed. I apologized to my parents for all the trouble I caused them growing up. I apologized to the good Lord for all the sins I committee and asked not only for his forgiveness but to release me from this living hell he'd subjected me to. As I lay there with my eyes closed I felt myself rolling to the other side of the bed as she lifted the king size mattress up with the strength of both Hercules and Zeus. I fell to the floor on the floor on the far side of the bed and though not a violent man only wished for a gun so I could put this poor creature who was intent on driving me crazy out of her misery.

The next morning I woke up tired and rest broken. She however, seemed fine and with all the etiquette of Queen Elizabeth told me it was an ailment that has affected her her whole life known as night terrors.

And it was from that day on that I never took her seriously. I now called her Mary Todd after Abraham Lincoln's wife who was known to be mentally insane.

The Text

I have since moved since our last correspondence. In a rush to get away I took he first thing available, a studio apartment over a garage facing an alley. It's hardly anything to write home about but it's peaceful. There is no drama and there is no chaos.

I can write in peace, turn up the music, and watch basketball. Yes there is cable television. The re refrigerator stays full and more importantly in the year and a half since I've been here not one utility has been shut off for lack of payment. Jewel and I still talk and up until today I was still under her spell but I made short work of that as she is still very much insane as you will see.

One day I was sitting writing when I heard my phone. It was her and the text read, 'I am having problems with Keith.'

I had long since stopped caring about Keith because I knew when she decided that she was going to take control and being both lazy and narcissistic I knew that it was a done deal. We could chalk up another Black male.

The fact of the matter is that she has no concept or understanding of all the different dynamics that it takes to raise a child yet alone a Black male. And so I turned a deaf eye to the entire situation.

I remember a football coach telling me that she had to first release him from her before he could ever coach him. I never told Jewel that because I feared for the coach. A few months ago Keith didn't make the basketball team. Now Keith stands six four and weighs around two ten and is easily the tallest boy on his basketball team. Well that was last year. I went to one of his games and watched the whole game. Keith did so as well from the bench. He the tallest was the twelfth and last man off the bench. But this year she called me.

"Would you believe that the school is predominantly Black and there are no Blacks on the basketball team."

She seemed enraged. Now accustomed to her frequent outbursts I just wondered who was going to reap the wrath or better yet who was she going to jail tonight. You could call her names today and the next thing you knew you were in jail for making terroristic threats.

"There are no Blacks on the team," I repeated trying to put things in perspective.

"No. That white bastard didn't put any Blacks on the team."

"None?"

"Not a one. But you know I'm going to the school tomorrow."

I didn't know if I should call ahead and at least get the coach a clean blanket and pillow for his stay in jail but I had long ago found out that more often than not she was delusional and created a scenario that best suited her needs for something that didn't go according to plan in her eyes.

Thinking about it I thought it best to wait a day or two and speak to Keith and get a more accurate picture of what she'd just told me. Now that is not to say that I didn't believe her but after the ballroom dancing incident, and the I'm going Christmas shopping with Rhonda and mommy I thought better of just swallowing her own unique twist on reality.

I no longer thought that I was the focal point of her lying. By now I had come to the summation that she was sick. I still loved her but I knew she was quite insane. The lies were no longer deliberate but were random and popped up more and more frequently and for no apparent reason After all, why would anyone call me and tell me that in an all-Black school a white coach would deliberately leave all the Black kids off the team. Sure, it's happened but now salary and tenure was based on winning percentage. I paused. I think I'd better talk to Keith before I gave any credibility to her latest story.

"I have company," I lied. "I'll call you back," I said.

Why me I asked myself. A couple of days later she stopped by and asked me to ide over to the house with her. I agreed. Keith was home.

"You playing ball?" I asked.

"Nah."

"Why not?"

"I missed tryouts."

"Why did you miss tryouts?"

"Well, last year I missed the first day of tryouts and made the team so I figured it was okay."

"Oh," I replied. "Tell me something. Is your team all-white?"

Keith looked at me like I was crazy.

"No, there ain't no white kids even on the team."

I never said anything. I didn't want to go to jail.

"Bay, you ready to go?"

"When you are." I replied.

A Basketball Scholarship

Humor me for a minute and understand that I use writing as therapy. And I fear that if I didn't that there's a good chance I would fall prey to my surroundings and lose my mind. It is true that I profess to be a teacher and an educator as I taught for a good may years in different capacities and in those years I have come to realize that there are a many teaching styles and methods. However, most rely on discipline, practice and repetition. That is a concept or skill is introduced. It is then practiced and then repeated until it is honed, learned and it becomes memorized. In the case of a skill such as basketball countless hours of practice are put in on a particular set of skills such as ball handling or shooting free throws. It takes years and countless hours of practice before a division I basketball player has the skills necessary to start and play for a division I school.

It takes a fair amount of dedication, desire and motivation to play and be proficient at any level. I explained this to Keith and he seemed to understand. And we both understood at the that moment and although he had the physical attributes he wasn't the least bit interested in putting forth the effort needed to be proficient at basketball.

And when the other kids were outside playing Keith would sit alone in the dark in the basement. At first I prompted

Jewel to force him to go out and socialize but she wouldn't. Not trying to engage her and bring the wrath of Satan down on my head I let it go. A few weeks later the kids would be out in the driveway playing basketball. And again Keith would be sitting in the dark down in the basement. And again I approached Jewel.

"Jewel have you had that boy tested?"

And why did I ask that?

"Yes I have and he was skipped. My son is very bright. Let me do mine okay? I don't need shit from you," she yelled.

I could see where this was going and tucked my tail between my legs and headed downstairs. Sitting down in the dark I thought back to North Carolina when she pleaded with me to come and help with her boys. They would soon be teenagers and she needed help. I jumped at the chance. It's what I had been doing most of my adult life. It was another chance to make a difference and now this. I laid down and went to sleep.

The next morning I heard her coming down the steps.

"Bay give me a dollar so Keith can get to school."

I couldn't believe my ears and wanted to say I thought you had you and yours but said nothing to this old crazy chick.

A few days later Jewel's Uncle Donnie stopped by the house. Quite the nice fellow he marveled at Keith's height at which time Jewel beaming with pride commented, "Yes. The doctor said when he was born he might be seven feet. I'm just hoping he gets a basketball scholarship to go to college."

I gasped. She was truly delusional to think that he would *earn* a basketball scholarship for sitting in the dark alone in the basement.

A huge fan of Barack Obama I wondered if she went so far as to think he practiced and honed his oratory shills or if he sat in the basement in the dark and then suddenly appeared on the world stage in front of millions a gifted orator. I knew she was delusional then. And after working with Special Education students I knew that something was amiss. Keith was autistic or something. And everyone that came through recognized it. But not Jewel and I soon gave up trying to make her aware. Her own mental illness would erupt if there were any discussion of her son was brought up.

But today I got a phone call. Keith is now a junior in high school.

"Bay I went to Keith's school today to meet with his teacher's to talk about college and they're saying that Keith needs to be tested. They say he has trouble concentrating."

I made no comment.

Snapback, Schemes and Dreams and Other Shit...

It's Sunday afternoon and a pleasant one at that. After scorching temperatures the last few days which drove my dear Jewel from a pleasant, easygoing woman back to being a crazed loony whose every other sentence contained the word hot.

"Bay it's hot. Bay?"

I didn't know what she wanted me to say or do but the weatherman had been saying the thing all week and my responding to the obvious made no sense to me. Besides my expending energy agreeing with her as sweat dripped down and hung on my balls before dripping down my legs making it looked as though I had peed on myself.

Hell, I knew it was hot but I wasn't going to entertain the idea especially when I had long time ago come to the realization that there were certain things which I in all my greatness had absolutely no control over. I had long been a believer in the Serenity Prayer and transcendental meditation. I accepted what was and then chose to put myself in another state of mind. I was cool at least that's what I chose to think and as long as I thought I was cool then I was.

Well, that was up until Jewel purposely or maybe just because she was a woman and was emotionally unstable as most women are reminded me once again that it was hot. Why she thought I was unaware of this I do not know. And the hotter it got the meaner she became. As you know I've been attending anger management meetings with the idea of controlling my anger but the more I went the angrier she became. Most of her anger was channeled at my drinking—a habit which had long ago been permanently etched in stone and which aggravated her to no end although I don't know why.

"Bay it"s hot. Bay…"

Again I didn't know why she felt a need to state the obvious but then you have to know Jewel. The thermostat read ninety something degrees and the heat index stated that it was in the hundreds and the humidity was almost unbearable. But she obviously thought that I was unaware of that so she told me it was hot repeatedly.

"Bay it's hot. Bay…"

In any case, I was doing my best to have some patience. The fact that I was and had been out of work for close to three weeks was really beginning to bother me and the heat and the fact that I was broke didn't make things any better.

I'd been working towards a store for as long as I'd been in Pittsburgh so I'd never felt absolutely destitute but I was becoming more and more desperate as the days went on. I'd been to a couple of flea markets in the past two weeks but both were full of Jed Clampett's relatives and I saw no real outlet for The Wu Tang Clan or Malcolm's cds in these venues and so I sought to hit the streets.

Now Pittsburgh is known to have its ghettoes just like every other major city and I sought to hit the worst ones. Now I grew up in New York and have frequented Harlem and Bed-Stuy and have been to Baltimore and D.C.'s notorious ghettoes and have even been to London's Brixton and returned from each saying 'thank God for the suburbs'.

And after a couple of drinks I was pretty sure that I was ready for Pittsburgh's Aliquippa section. My wife was angry as usual. (I don't know what her particular reason was on this day. She has a large bag in which she sticks her hand in—like a lottery—for slips in which there are different reasons to be angry and she seldom tells me the reason but I knew she hardly wanted to go). You see one of her favorite pastimes is sleeping and she could sleep seventeen or eighteen hours a day if I'd let her. And the mere reason that I wouldn't allow was reason in itself. You see my dear wife who I love deeply could sleep a full night and wake up in the morning have a ten minute conversation with me and with no remorse tell me she's tired and needs to take a nap.

Anyway, after much coercing I convinced her to go against her will and I was pleasantly surprised at how warm and friendly the people were in spite of the conditions. In New York or North Carolina, Aliquippa would have been considered suburbia. But here it was considered the ghetto. In any case, I had a case of New Era caps, which sold for about thirty-five dollars a cap, but being that we were on the street we agreed to sell them for fifteen or twenty.

The first place we came to was a bar where we met a young brother about twenty-five or thirty named Smid who lost his mind when he saw the hats.

"Man I can sell all these hats. And they official too. C'mon let me ride with you and you gonna hook me up if I sell these hats for you. Right? I sell six hats you gonna give me one right?"

My wife who is used to directing and running the show took over.

"Yeah we gonna look out. You just sell the hats."

And sell he did. Directing her, Smid took her from bar-to-bar and project-to-project selling hats. It was beautiful and the money started rolling in all of which Jewel stuck in her bra. I didn't think this was safe at first as my wife is not the most heavenly endowed and I worried about the money falling straight through and being lost.

She claims she wears a 38C but I know women and their bra sizes because I used to sell women's bras before I began selling hats and in her case the cup size is at best wishful thinking. Now, as I said before I love my wife but after thirty years at looking at her breasts I can tell you that she's somewhere between a training bra and a 34 with no substantial cup size to speak of. But never really being a breast man I could care less. What I do like are ass and hips and she's got enough in both areas to keep me smiling even if it's hot and she's angry and won't let me indulge.

Anyway, we sold for about two hours and Smid must have sold about ten or twelve hats an hour and every time he'd ask how many he'd sold in hopes of getting a free hat she'd tell him he had six more to go. The boy wasn't the brightest star in the sky but he had to sell at least twenty hats in route to his free hat and she still told him he had six to go. I had to bite a hole in my tongue to keep from laughing but I let her handle it and when he got out she'd given him all of two hats for his efforts while she pocketed over seven or eight hundred dollars. Being that I was part of the management team I said little although I knew it was a travesty.

By eight-thirty we were back on the road and heading for Pittsburgh when she dove back into her lottery bag of angry thoughts and dug out another reason to be angry but that was short-lived as she saw a way to fix her account and make it balanced. So whereas Sid got two hats and she got close to eight hundred dollars for two hours of driving I got zip except the comment the next day that, 'all I am is your jitney driver'.

Well, being that I just graduated from my Anger Management class with a graduate degree that they don't give to just anyone but because I live with Cruella Devil I was given the highest of the Anger Management degrees because everyone that knows my wife knows exactly what I'm up against.

The night despite the negativity made me feel good though. Once again I knew that I could rely on my own creativity and drive and make it on my own in the streets that my parents had tried so hard to protect me from.

Still, it angered me that my folks still had so much to learn. I would often ask my father while we would be watching the NBA why so many of our athletes would run around endorsing other people's sneakers and clothing lines instead of creating and endorsing our own. Michael Jordan was a prime example. He single-handedly made Nike the largest sneaker company in the world and it just seemed ludicrous that he and a few of his peers wouldn't get together to endorse their logos on a brand that they owned.

I never understood. And I never could quite grasp why our people would go down fighting over a logo or brand that they had absolutely no stock or affiliation with. To know that you are being targeted by marketing representatives on Fifth Avenue that have no contact, no respect and would move from their lily White homes in the suburbs if they thought the likes of you were attempting to move not next door but into the neighborhood is itself reason enough not to don a logo made popular by them and targeted just for you.

I noticed a couple of years ago how New Era Cap Company had eliminated my father's two dollar golf cap with the snapback where one size could fit all in lieu of the fitted cap which now came in different sizes depending on the size of one's head and was now charging thirty-five dollars for a hat which in all honesty did the same thing as the two dollar snapback and that is to cover the head from the elements. I thought it was a great marketing ploy and Blacks, who have little or no money and quick to get a hold of anything that's expensive and different are the last to question who and why they are purchasing something of this nature. And so here I was with the ever popular fitted caps and they ate them up with all the gusto and aplomb of a man at his last supper but what was interesting to me was that in the year or so the fashion had once again changed and now they were asking for the rejected snapbacks at the new improved price of twenty dollars. I had a few but when I ran out I wondered where my father had tossed his old golf cap he used to go out and rake the leaves in.

And as I looked around there was my beautiful wife, who I love dearly saying "Bay it's hot. Bay? And shuffling through her bag of slips looking for another reason to be angry.

Bay

Even though it was a text I could hear her familiar whine.

'Bay! Keith's giving me problems.'

In the five or six years I had known this quiet unassuming kid I had never known him to give anyone any problems but knew that my Jewel was the queen of drama and could cause havoc in heaven but I humored her.

'What's wrong?'

'He won't let me give him a suppository.'

I don't know how long it took for me to respond. Here he was sixteen years old standing all of six foot four and more than two hundred pounds and she wanted him to take his pants down so she could stick her finger up his butt and give him an enema. Need I say more?

It's Deep

My father was on his death bed in Maryland. I was only hoping I would arrive in time. Jewel's mother volunteered to take me and I was grateful. Jewel and I were in our first or second year of marriage and it was no easy going. We are argued constantly over the house and her not being a clean individual. It was not unusual for her to come home from work and run to the bathroom and leave her panties or shoes in the middle of the floor. This may have been a pet peeve of mine but that along with the fact that for a year or so we worked minutes from each other and would ride back and forth together. When we'd arrive home our second job started. There was the cooking, the cleaning, the washing of the clothes and more to do. And then there was the matter of having a child and the added responsibility of having children and their care and guidance.

I having two children from a previous marriage knew that this was my first priority and the first thing I would do was tend to their needs. We'd sit down and I'd inquire about their day, before moving on and asking them about their schoolwork and sitting down and going over their homework and any future tests. I'd go over areas where they were having difficulty and help in any way I could.

Perhaps I married too late in life. Perhaps I wasn't very adaptive to this new lifestyle. Perhaps I couldn't adapt but there was no inclination to tidy up, to cook or to inquire about the children and no reference ever made to schoolwork from Jewel. And so I took on the added extra burden of setting up a chore list for the three boys which they adhered to pretty well and bought a book series for pre-teens which consisted of thirteen books. They were required to read ten pages a night and then come and tell us what they read. As Jewel showed no interest I was forced to listen to them tell me what they read on most nights. They then had to keep a journal. I didthis with the hopes of improving their reading and writing skills. As I told you before after teaching in New York and North and South Carolina I know that you can't rely on the school system to educate your children. And that was okay if she'd lent a hand in some of the other areas but she refused to do that as well.

When the washing machine broke I bought a new one but she never washed clothes. I washed hers and her sons. Her excuse, "I don't go down there," meaning the basement. So, along with trying to provide a home life for the boys and educate them I was responsible for the general upkeep of the home in general.

Now Jewel was a fabulous cook and could whip up a meal in a manner of minutes but only if the whim hit her which wasn't too frequently. When she did nine times out ten it was vegetable free unless it was a stir fried dish which came with vegetables like broccoli and bean shoots. Aside from that it was a vegetable free diet for the most part.

I suffered after having a first wife that would come home after work and fix a balanced meal each and every night for the past twenty five years. I shared the cooking duties in my first marriage abut now was forced to cook ninety per cent of the time if I wanted to live. I lost fifty pounds in my first year in Pittsburgh. The boy's diet consisted of hot dogs, peanut butter and jelly sandwiches and cereal.

I talked, bribed and argued with Jewel to try something new but she told me in no uncertain words that 'mommy told you I didn't cook or clean'. And she had at that so I sat back once again dazed and confused and wondered how I had gotten into this shit. Here I was in my fifties. My children were grown and I kept hearing my first wife's voice telling me how now that the kids were gone we would have peace and would build a fence around the patio so we could sit around naked and sip Pina Coladas and when we got bored we could shoot up to New York and do a little shopping or fly down to the Bahamas for New Years. And as much as I loved Jewel I knew then that I'd made a mistake of magnanimous proportions. Jewel had sold me a lie. She'd given me the impression that she'd had it all together in North Carolina but in reality her life was in shambles and I'd bought into her lies hook, line and sinker.

I truly believe her mother tried to warn me but I had been too egotistical to listen. She told me in no uncertain terms that she couldn't handle her money. I was later to find this to be all too true. She owed one hundred and twenty five thousand dollars on her student loan which she defaulted on and had bad credit. There were overdraft statements coming in daily. The utilities would be turned off every couple of months. And though she had a fairly good salary—sixty thousand a year—she was constantly taking out payday advances at exorbitant interest rates. So, she stayed broke and owed everyone in Pittsburgh. I soon came to find out that no one; absolutely no one would lend her money because of her reputation for not paying back money she'd borrowed. It was truly a sad situation and in the year and a half that I dated her I had no inclination that she was living a double life.

I can remember her mother coming by to visit and going to use the bathroom but instead of coming back to rejoin the conversation in the living room she went to the kitchen, picked up the broom and returned to the bathroom and began sweeping and muttering about how nasty it was. I had never been so embarrassed in all my life but Jewel played it off as she always did saying,

'That's just how mommy is. You have to get to know mommy.' But mommy and I were in agreement. Jewel was lazy and nasty. Her sister came over a few weeks later and made a similar comment saying she didn't know why Jewel was so nasty and again I dropped my head.

Our kitchen was another story in itself. We had no kitchen floor. I was saving to have it done and I eventually did but at the time her mother visited we no kitchen floor and her mother said, 'You'd better replace that floor before you end up in the basement.'

Now I don't know if Jewel heard any of these messages or simply chose to ignore them but I believed in prioritizing things but her financial situation was in such flux that both her mother and I who were both more adept at handling money volunteered to get her finances in order. She dismissed both of our attempts to help as her mother looked at the kitchen floor. Meanwhile, I went to the refrigerator to grab something to eat. There was no kitchen floor and there was no food. And where was Jewel? In the bedroom getting dressed to go the casino...

I had long since grown tired of her erratic and delusional behavior. It just didn't make any sense to me. How could she say she love not only me and her son and not put any food in the fridge or live in such a fashion. A friend of mine when I told him of Jewel's behavior asked me if I loved her enough to put up with her mental illness and for the first two years I did. But I knew now that it was time to go before I too ended up mentally ill or in jail for murder.

I'd gotten paid that day too. His father had already commented long before I arrived that he wasn't paying child support or committing to being a father but I never thought that Jewel would decline her responsibilities as well. But that she did on so numerous an occasions that that became the norm whether than the exception. My father used to call it warehousing instead of parenting and I agree. Some don't know how to and she admitted so but Jewel was no ordinary woman and had the intellect to be mother of the year but and though she loved her son she chose not to put any effort into childrearing.

And so she left the house and headed to the casino. Now I could have bought groceries but I was contributing my every check but the fact that she would and could ignore the needs of the house and her son to go give money to the casino when her mother had just said fix the floor or wind up in the basement. Wow! And then I realized if she ignored the conventional wisdom of her mother, the quiet crying out of her son then why would what I thought matter.

I started buying dry goods, like peanut butter nabs, cookies and sardines and put them in the cupboard in the basement and now lived and was determined to move out the first chance I could even though I so wanted her to wake up and turn things around.

It was funny though. If I asked her to fix my commuter or design a book cover I received the usual whining.

'Ah bay. Do I have to?' And minutes later it would be fixed. But feed her son, buy toilet paper or buy wash cloths and towels she just could not do. It was almost as if this were out of the realms of this world.

I drank a lot in those days just to keep my sanity. I was in hell! I was working with the county then with Children Youth and Families and recounted the fact that the children had no beds and what their diet consisted of and was told that as a mandated reporter I had the obligation to report neglect and abuse of any child but I loved my wife and couldn't have these children taken away and so I never spoke of it again.

It's funny though. My first or second year into the marriage I took the oldest child, her nephew, (who I utterly adored), with me to North Carolina. He was a bright kid with a beautiful personality and an amiable smile that endeared him to everyone he met. But he happened to be in a tough situation. Both his parents were crack addicts and he had a hard time understanding why his mother, Jewel's sister did not want him. In turn, he would act out fighting and getting suspended from school at every turn. His situation was commonplace and I took this as a chance to give something back as I had been an addict for close to some twenty five years.

In any case, I had recovered and now sought to walk the straight and narrow if only I had a mate that was willing to let me. I hated addiction of any kind and to marry a woman that was an addict was beyond the realm of my thinking. Furthermore Jewel was in denial and still is 'til this day. But at the time I had had enough. And so I packed my bags and decided to go back to North Carolina to ponder my present situation. I was at a crossroads. I truly loved Jewel despite her mental illness but didn't know if I loved her enough to put my own sanity at risk and she was certainly testing me. As Travis was suspended and she was at her wit's ends she permitted him to go with me. (I do believe this was her way of assuring herself that I would come back or a way at least to stay in touch).

So, we left with no thought of returning. I enrolled him in school and was soon back in my comfort zone. He obviously felt something he hadn't felt before and the days would end with us sitting around the dining table sharingstories of our day. Following dinner as was our custom we played a board game or two before resigning to the living room for a movie or just to continue talking.

It was fast approaching Christmas and we were putting up the tree and decorating the house when my daughter asked Travis what he wanted for Christmas. He dropped his head and we all knew that she'd struck a nerve.

"Do you know what auntie got us last Christmas?"

"No. What she get you."

"We got I.O.U.'s."

We were speechless.

My ex-wife, who worked part time and had never forgiven me for leaving me for Jewel turned and stared at me, I dropped my head. She looked at me as if to say, 'and this is what you left me for?'

He soon made friends with the neighborhood kids and whereas I was still under Jewel's throes and didn't know if I was returning to Pittsburgh Travis knew he wasn't going back.

I understood his reservations about not returning. At thirteen he had for the first time experienced what he had always longed for; a stable home environment and had fallen in love with it. Me, well I had fallen in love with Jewel and stable home life or not I was crazy about her. So, when the time came and she asked whether I had made up my mind or not I was still unsure. But Travis had made up his mind. He was not going back.

"Let me speak to him."

I handed the phone to him and watched as he dropped his head.

"You get your little ass packed and get ready to come back home. Do you hear me?"

"Yes, Aunt Darling," he said before handing the phone back to me and kicking and storming back to his room.

"Bay, I'll be there tomorrow."

"Listen Travis. I don't know what went on between you and your aunt but nobody here has done a thing to you so don't walk through kicking and cursing and mad at the world." I told Travis the tears dripping from his eyes.

"Let me speak to him bay."

I gave the phone to him but I understood. Better than anyone else I understood.

The next day, a Friday North Carolina was expecting snow, a rare occurrence when jewel called. I told Travis to answer the phone. He did and put it on speaker. It had snowed earlier that day. And as it was with snowfall in North Carolina it was a rare dusting not even covering the street.

"How is it Travis?" Jewel asked. "Is there a lot of snow?"

"Yeah Aunt Darling. It's pretty deep."

The Old Double Standard

Here are some things I knew after I got over my addiction to drugs. I knew that I had to move twice as fast to make up for lost time. I was focused.

I knew that I would never let anyone get in my way again and that I would never fall prey to any substance again. And a lot of people including Jewel ask me how I can drink after being a drug addict. I don't know and can't explain it to her but my constitution has never been stronger and I have too many other goals and objectives that I must now reach to let anything distract me. I've always been driven but never more than I am now.

I have a strong faith and belief in the Lord Jesus Christ and I know that I would have never been able to overcome my demons if it hadn't been for my faith in Him and his belief in me. And with Him by my side I know there is nothing on this earth that I cannot accomplish with Him by my side.

So, when Jewel said rather nonchalantly that she wanted me to give up drinking and my female friends I'd know all my life I agreed. Drinking was not a problem except that it acted as truth serum for me and where I would bite my tongue and gloss over much of her madness when I was sober and she could maintain her ineptness when I drank I managed to pinpoint all her flaws. So, the drinking in her eyes had to go. And because of her ineptness everyone else became a threat. In all actuality the only threat to her was herself. But she never understood that and no matter what I did or said she never understood that she held a unique place in my heart. Everyone else did but not her. But I agreed to give up my friends, (although she kept friends and former lovers), and alcohol and she give up gambling.

She agreed but had no intentions of following through on the agreement and the first inkling she had to go she went. It was then I recognized that gambling wasn't just a hobby but an addiction. She being in denial and not knowing the physiognomies or characteristics of addiction did not see herself as an addict because she did not go each and every payday. What she didn't realize was that there are many types of addict. The worst addiction is perhaps the daily user. There is also the binge drinker who may go for extended periods of time without using and then may go off and use forgetting any and all responsibilities until there is nothing left. There is also the functional addict who will maintain his or her job and responsibilities but will nevertheless continue this behavior for many years within the confines of being functional. There are tell-tale signs of addiction which even a daily users can mask for long periods of time depending on their self-esteem and other variables which would have them hide their addiction. But

Jewel was not too smart and the fact that she was in denial and not really in full control of either her addiction or her life it was somewhat easy to see for everyone but her. As I mentioned earlier her mother had a chance to spend some time together on a ride to see my father who was in hospice at the time. On the way there her mother confided to me that she was a lot like her father in several ways. Neither she nor her father could handle money and both were at best degenerate gamblers which is the primary reason for her mother not lending her money. She didn't want to expand on her daughter's problems but gave several rather humorous stories of what she went through with her husband and his constant mismanagement of money when he was alive.

"I made him bring me every check or we would never had anything. I remember I went away one weekend and left him the money to the pay the electric bill when I came home the lights were off and he was sitting there in the dark I said M. didn't I tell you to pay the electric bill at which time he turned to me and said I was wondering why I had this extra money."

I wondered if her addictive personality was genetic. But when I recounted what her mother had shared with me the only she took from it was that I should do as her father had done and turn over my check every other week to her. I was turning the majority of it over now and we weren't making any forward progress so I looked at her like she was crazy which she was.

There were other signs that she was an addict and mentally ill which often go hand-in-hand and I've known enough addicts to know. But the most obvious signs manifested themselves in the fact that she would lie to hide her addiction. There was the 'I'm going ballroom dancing' and another instance when she told me, 'I'm going Christmas shopping' when I went down to the casino and caught her red handed spinning the wheel. After a while it all came into plain view. She couldn't pay bills and ever get ahead because she was like her father a degenerate gambler.

Now I didn't have any friends in Pittsburgh and anyone that I talked to I was sleeping with so after a while I gave up the whole notion of talking to anyone. It got so bad that one of my clients called to check on me on my work phone when I was in the hospital for the better part of a week with high blood pressure and she called the woman to ask if I were fucking her.

On another occasion I met a woman I had known for more than forty years, (since I was eight or nine years old). We'd grown up together and gone to college. Anyway, I hadn't seen her in more than thirty years and we embraced at my uncle's funeral and I introduced her to Jewel. I was glad to see her and we exchanged numbers. When she called Jewel promptly answered and told her not to call her husband again. Other friends called from time-to-time and were told the same thing. I was forbidden to get rides from co-workers or go out with them after work. And in an attempt to do anything I could to make my failing marriage work I gave up drinking and talking to people.

On the way to see my father I brought up Jewel's jealousy to her mother.

"Her father was the same way. It used to drive me crazy."

"So, what did you do?"

"I ignored it."

So, I took her advice but six months later I had still not had a drink or spoken to my friends and felt like I was under house arrest with no idea the crime while she maintained her relationship with her old flame Jean Marquis whom she claims took her to Brazil for a couple of years, (but that's another story).

In any case she has never cut off ties with him or gambling even though in our arrangement those were the terms. I eventually went back to doing as I pleased but the jealousy began to manifest itself in maddening proportions. She didn't want me to talk to my kid's mother but she interacted with her ex. No females were acceptable and she dislike all of my male friends as well pointing out each one's flaws as if there were such a thing as flawless people.

She would find something wrong with all of them even though none of them has to this day lied and cheated me as she had.

At one point I was talking to my daughter and was told, 'Okay get off the phone. That's enough.' That's when I knew all the bricks weren't in the wagon. Well, I knew before then but once again she let me know that despite my efforts I didn't have the type of help she needed.

It eventually came to a head when my friend Beatrice said she was coming to town. I hadn't seen Bea in a couple of years and prior to that it'd been close to thirty years. A couple of years before she called to tell me she was coming to town and wanted to take me out for my birthday. I was elated and we arranged to meet at Joe's Crab Shack. So, not to leave Jewel out and so she wouldn't be jealous I invited her to come along. Beatrice met us with her two children and we sat down to reminisce. No more than five minutes had gone by and Jewel came down with something and went and sat in the car. I excused myself and took her home. Funny thing but as soon as she got home she was fine.

Two years later Bea called to tell me she would be in town so I agreed to meet her but did not tell Jewel so she could sabotage this time as well and we met with her friend Pastor Tookes and another brother I had gone to college with.

The evening was enjoyable and it was good seeing my college buddies. But my enjoyable evening out was short-lived. When I got home I was met with…

"You fuckin' bastard, I know you were out with that white girl."

Used to her madness I walked to the bedroom without uttering a word and climbed into bed pulling the cover over my head. This only seemed to enrage her even more and she proceeded to call me every name in the book and would continually flick the light switch on so I couldn't get any sleep. I'd turn it off. She'd turn it on until I had had enough and broke the light. I then proceeded to push her out of the room. I don't know why I did this since there wasn't a door in the house that worked properly and could be locked. She then started to flail at me. I grabbed a handful of her hair hoping to keep her at bay and of course she called the police who handcuffed me and took me to the hospital to check on my hand which was bleeding profusely before carting me off to jail. The older of the two suggested that I leave which was beginning to become a recurring thought in my mind and as I sat in that jail cell I asked myself the same thing.

I'd done what her mother suggested and tried to ignore her jealous fits of rage but that only incensed her more. By this time I had no place to go. My ex-wife who had all but begged me to come to my senses the first two years had moved on and was now involved in a troubled relationship of her own had given up hope. A day or later I was let out only to have her drop all charges in court a few weeks later.

In court, I once again came to the conclusion that she was quite mad.

"Mrs. Brown did the defendant put his hands on you?" the judge asked.

"My son answered the phone," Jewel replied.

The judge looked at the prosecuting attorney who looked at the defense lawyer who looked at the court clerk who looked at me. I in turned looked at the judge and wanted to say, 'See. And you detained me. You should have put a straight coat on her and 302'd her ass. She's the one that's crazy. I deserve reparations for my night in jail at the hands of this crazy chick.' But I said nothing. The judge who figured that perhaps Jewel hadn't understood the question repeated it. A lot of good that's gonna do I said to myself.

"Mrs. Brown did the defendant put his hands on you?" the judge asked.

"My son answered the phone," Jewel replied.

The judge paused before slamming his gavel down.

"Case dismissed," he said.

"Thank you your honor," I said before turning and walking out of the courtroom. Outside on the street Jewel was all smiles.

"I told you I got this," she said to me. But my mind was elsewhere. This was my fifth or sixth time I'd been to court over something along these same lines and each time she'd had the charges dropped. I was tired of this and knew that we could not co-exist in the same household. So, I decided that until I could move the best way to work this out was that neither of us should have friends of the opposite sex in our marriage. She seemed only to happy with this plan. And so I relegated myself to talking to family and no one else.

Months passed and in the interim one of her nephews robbed the house and stole my phone in the process so I was without a phone.

"Bay I'm gonna leave my phone with you so you have a phone."

"Okay."

Around twelve that afternoon she received a text and the name lit up. It was Jean Marquis. I ignored it. After all, I couldn't blame her for him trying to reach her although if she had been serious she could have blocked his number. Still, I ignored it. After all, I hardly cared anymore and to bring it up would have only caused more problems and I was about eliminating the drama. My sole concern was getting away from her and all the madness.

Five minutes later the phone rang. A man's voice was on the other end.

"Hello."

"Hello. Is Jewel there?"

"No, she isn't. May I take a message?"

"No, I'm just returning her call."

"Oh, okay," I said hurt to no end. "She's at work. Why don't you give her a call at the office? Do you have her number?"

"Thanks man. Yeah I got it."

Later he texted again.

I was hurt to no end that she had given me her word again and once again broken it. When she called I told her he'd

called. She played it off like it was nothing and it probably wasn't but the fact that she'd lied to me again hurt deeply.

I always figured that marriage was trust and if you couldn't trust your mate then you really didn't have anything to base your marriage on. Not long after I moved and she came to visit frequently and came to stay on the weekends.

I was free or so I thought. Jewel, never bashful or shy came with the same demands she always had. No women! I didn't really have a problem with that as she was the only woman I had ever truly loved and after six years I was more in love with her than I ever was.

She'd stop by the house after work on most days if not to do anything more than chit chat and I was always glad to see her.

On one particular day, I begged her to take me to Wendy's to get a milk shake.

"Ah bay do I have to?" was the standard response. And so it was on this day. (I could never understand that since she did most of the requesting and there wasn't anything I wouldn't do for her but let me ask and I'd end up begging and pleading.)

In any case, she left my apartment and in the manner of three blocks she had a bladder attack. This wasn't uncommon. I'm just glad she made it. She jumped out of the car giving her phone and keys which I promptly put in my pocket. After ordering dinner for she and her son she dropped me off back at the house and headed home.

Now as is my ritual I came up and was just about to empty my pockets when I heard a text. Funny thing though it wasn't my phone. Digging in my pocket she'd forgotten to take her phone. I took it out and there was Jean Marquis texting. Being of a curious nature I opened it to see what it was he wanted now. I was shocked to find over a hundred texts from this man to my wife. This is the same wife who forbade me from talking or texting any female friends. And she was adamant about it too.

The more I read the angrier I got. I was not only angry. I was hurt beyond belief. I had been duped and deceived and lied to once again. Reading the text I read things like, 'Baby let me pick you up and take you to dinner? I promise I won't touch you.' And she replied, 'Are you treating?' And it looked like a go but Keith came home and she replied. 'I'm sorry my baby just walked in the house. Maybe another time... I love you.' I couldn't believe the words before me and it got worse.

Months before any of this occurred I told you of our excursion to Aliquippa to sell hats for twenty dollars apiece although they were twice that. Well, in my haste to leave I'd picked out a dozen for myself with a street value of somewhere around two hundred and forty dollars but forgotten them so I called her and asked them if she'd bring them on her next trip over to which she agreed.

"Sure bay I'll put them in the car now."

A week later I was still asking her to bring the hats. At first it was, "I forgot I'll bring them tomorrow."

Reading the texts I was shook up over all the 'baby' and 'I love yous' but then I hit a text that read 'Are you interested in some brand new New Blank caps' to which he replied.

'How much?'

'I'll sell you a dozen for twenty five dollars.'

'Are you serious? And you say they're brand new?'

'Would I lie to you?'

'Meet me at the busway.'

My hats that were worth two hundred and forty dollars she sold for twenty five dollars. By this time I was damn near in tears. One hundred and twenty eight texts to an ex after sending me to jail because of her own jealousy. I couldn't read anymore but was smart enough to forward the texts to my phone before getting up to go to the liquor store to try to drown my sorrows. My eyes get misty just writing about it. I walked and wondered. I wondered how to respond or better yet if I should respond at all. My phone rang.

"Bay, do you have my phone."

"No. I mean yeah but not on me I left it at the house. I'm not at home."

"Where are you?"

"I'm at Edgewood."

"What are you doing at Edgewood?"

"Just walking."

"Did you go through my phone?"

"No. I have no reason to do that."

"Yes, you did."

"And what if I did? You can go through mine. We are married. I have no secrets to hide. Do you? Where are you? I thought you were coming back to spend the night."

"I don't know if I want to now."

"Well, that's up to you," I responded not knowing if I wanted her to or not.

Ten minutes later I approached my tiny apartment and saw her car out front. There was absolutely no way she could have driven home and gotten back that fast. Something must really be wrong I thought.

I put the pint of Paul Masson in the mailbox and headed up to the loft. I certainly knew not to drink in the mood I was in. Drinking was like truth serum and I surely didn't want to lose it. No. I would just let it play out.

She was sitting on the couch when I arrived; phone in one hand scrolling down the page. I sat on the bed and stared at her for the next hour as she read every text panic in her eyes. Now if you know Jewel you sometimes pray for her to just be quiet but on this night all she did was stare at her phone and read never saying a word. I inquired as to why she was so quiet. Always one to want to snuggle I called her to bed. For a while she refused. After a while she climbed into the bed. Minutes later she was fast asleep. I picked up her phone. Every message was still there except those she received from Jean Marquis. I couldn't understand why. If they had been innocent why she erase them? I was seething and still at a loss as to how I should approach the situation. She was stirring in her sleep and finally awoke.

"Bay could you turn off the lights and the music?"

I wanted her to hurt. I wanted her to feel the anguish that I was feeling. All the emotions of a man in love deceived again came cascading down on me. I'd gone downstairsand gotten the bottle and sipped liberally. I was hot but thought of the repercussions of doing something foolish. As she got up to use the bathroom I asked her.

"Jewel why did you sell my hats?"

"What hats? I didn't sell your hats. I didn't sell your hats. What are you talking about?"

"My hats. Read the texts you wrote them. And then you're cheating on me? You're meeting this guy and making plans to go to dinner?"

"We weren't married then."

"Perhaps I didn't get the memo but no one told me we were divorced."

"Why did you sell my hats?"

"I don't know what you're talking about."

She'd erased every text from him and I could see no reason to erase them if there had been no guilt. After all, there were texts on there from her ex-husband inquiring about their son. She left those as they were innocent enough. But her guilt exposed itself when she erased all of his texts.

"I handed my phone so she would stop denying the obvious. She stood without answering and, dressed quickly and left.

Several weeks later she invited to go with her to a conference in Harrisburg, Pennsylvania. I'd calmed downed some but still didn't appreciate this man calling and texting my wife and calling her baby and other terms of endearment. I explained this to her and asked her if her father would have permitted her mother to see men she used to sleep with. Any normal, logical married person would not conduct themselves in this manner but then

Jewel was not normal or logical and despite the fact that it upset me to no end she continued to stay in contact with this man. On the way back from Harrisburg she made it plain.

"I'm not going to hurt him by cutting him off," she screamed at me.

"But you don't mind hurting your husband," I asked her.

It was disturbing and the idea that I was not permitted to talk to women or have women visit me though it was purely platonic upset me to no end. I understood her being jealous but the idea that she could and I couldn't upset me to no end. And this fellow obviously meant more to her than her marriage to me.

"Go ahead and see your friends because I'm not going to hurt him."

I did just that but again I had to really question this marriage and this woman. I even went so far as to include a married friend of mine on the matter.

"I don't think it's a good idea to bring other people into your marriage," he told her but she just didn't get it.

Being that I'm damn near blind and always doing something I put my phone on talk and when I receive a text it will say the message aloud. This way I don't have to stop what I'm doing to answer the phone. So, we tested her proposal that I keep my friends and she keep hers, (although I didn't particularly care for that proposal).

A few weeks later, she was sitting on my bed watching television and I received a text from my best friend Beatrice that read 'I love you boo. Goodnight.'

I looked over at Jewel and wasn't sure if she was having a seizure or what. She turned three shades of crimson red. I was literally afraid to be in the same room and then she started spewing out things like, 'Oh, so she loves you?'

I suppose the old double standard didn't sit too well.

Respect Is Earned

When I first moved to Pittsburgh I had some grandiose ideas about my marriage and the way I was going to just blossom. After all I had the woman of my dreams and the sky was the limit. I knew if I had any success close to what I had in North Carolina we'd be fine. I saw so many possibilities and I think my enthusiasm was infectious. But the Pittsburgh mentality was quite a bit different.

Everyone in North Carolina had a hustle or a second job to supplement their income and Black folks were on the grind. Jewel commented on one of her many trips there that she had never seen so many Blacks driving Mercedes.

In Pittsburgh a blue collar town and one of the more depressed cities who lost its industry when both the steel mills and the coal mines moved overseas so you'd think you'd see more people hustling and trying to put a little cash in their pockets. But no…

Jewel was glad to have me here in the beginning and she like I saw unlimited possibilities in the beginning and with me there to her she could now see her dreams coming to fruition.

"Bay, do you see these weeds? Oh, I hate them."

Leading me by the hand, she walked me around the yard and showed me each and every weed.

"Oh, I just hate them,"

After the hour long tour I was well versed in what weed she hated, which ones she despised and which weeds she truly detested and not to let my baby suffer the emotional upheaval from these awful creatures invading her precious grass I decided to hire a landscaper. Now a great many of Pittsburgh's natives live in little more than hovels and you would think that they would be out there landscaping and the such to give them a better quality of life but after calling ten or fifteen and them either not showing or turning me down for one reason or another I knew that these people were not trying to get any money. I thought back to North Carolina where people would come through and go door-to-door the first day of spring handing out flyers advertising their little landscaping businesses.

And even though I had a brand new lawnmower it was cheaper to pay Mr. Martinez twenty dollars to cut, edge and pull the weeds every two weeks. When we wanted mums and perennials planted in the front yard we would give him an extra twenty and he'd mad a flower bed. But here they were spouting hundred dollar quotes after seeing the yard the work that needed to be done, giving a final estimate and then wouldn't show up to do the work.

After weeks I finally found someone to do the job and Jewel was only so happy to shell out five hundred dollars to get rid of those dastardly weeds. The only problem was the landscaper forgot to spray the weeds before covering the area with tarp and mulch and so the next spring the weeds attacked with a vengeance again and Jewel repeated what was now becoming her mantra as she got out of the tuck after work.

"I hate those fucking weeds."

133

Damn had changed to fucking and I knew it wouldn't be long before she'd be calling the Pentagon to get some drones to hone in on those weeds and so I started the process all over again. Only for the life of me, this time was even harder than the first and I couldn't find anyone.

It didn't take much to set Jewel off but I knew how she could get and the yard was one of many things she obsessed about. I don't know if I mentioned it before but one of the many ailments she suffered from was obsessive compulsive disorder. And one of the things she obsessed about was the yard.

I knew if something wasn't done soon there would all hell to pay. I was sitting on the front porch one day when I saw a couple when I noticed a couple of young white boys in a truck with a trailer and lawn mowers in the back. I dropped my beer and raced headlong into the street and threw myself in the street in front of the oncoming truck. I knew it was a risky move that could have possibly cost me my life but just the thought of having to live with Jewel for another day with the weeds taking over her every thought was an even more harrowing thought.

The two young men in the pickup truck pulled over to check on me. I got up brushed myself off and addressed the driver.

"You alright mister," the taller boy said.

"You cut grass," I gasped out of breath after the long run and dive.

"Yeah, we cut grass."

"Well, I need my grass cut but more importantly I have a weed problem that is my wife has a weed problem and is losing her mind over the invasion of weeds."

The younger man smiled.

"Yeah weeds are like having a pest control problem."

"No son, you don't understand my wife doesn't mind pests. Maggots, swarms of gnats and vermin are okay and all part of the southwestern landscape according to her but weeds are somewhat akin to the anti-Christ in her book. My sanity is in jeopardy. Can you help me son?"

"Well, we can certainly take a look. Let's see what we have here."

"Let me call my wife so she can tell you exactly what she wants. By the way I'm Mr. Brown and you are?"

"Paul. Just call me Paul."

"Okay Paul. Let me get her."

And here is where I was to make a mistake that I would live to regret although I had no idea at the time.

"Jewel! Jewel!"

"Yeah Bay. Why are you yelling?" she said bending over and pulling one of those hated weeds.

"Jewel this is Paul and he does yard work. Says he can get rid of those weeds."

Jewels eyes lit up and sparkled for the first time since her last scratch off.

"Just take him around and show him exactly him what you want done."

Jewel pointed to each and every weed as I watched from the kitchen window. I felt sorry for the young man as I'd taken the same tour on several occasions and knew that one weed looked just like the next but she was diligent in her hatred and made sure that she identified the crabgrass from the dandelions and made known her hatred for each. When it was over Paul looked at her quizzically and wondered the same thing I wondered. Were all the bricks in the wagon?

I came out to release the boy from this torture.

"So, what kind of price are we talking?"

"Well, Mr. Brown the way I see it the first time with the weeding and the planting the flowers and pruning the hedges I'd say thirty five dollars and then to come back every two weeks to cut the grass it'll be a flat twenty dollars."

"Sounds good to me Paul."

"Okay then Mr. Brown. I'll be back tomorrow morning."

It was bright and early Saturday morning before the birds were up I heard the steady buzz of hedge clippers accompanied by a lawn mower and went to peek out the window, sleep still in my eyes and was pleasantly surprised to see Paul and his co-worker hard at work. In an hour or so there came a knock at the door and I grabbed my wallet.

"Hold on fellas like me get my wife to check it out."

I grabbed Jewel who was still half asleep.

"Ah, bay just go and look."

"No, Jewel you won't wait until their gone and then start complaining about what they didn't do or what they missed. No. You go and see if they did everything you wanted them to do."

In fifteen minutes she was back in and I was surprised when I saw them packing their tools and equipment back in the trailer. These two teenagers had done something that in two years I hadn't been able to do. They passed one of Jewel's inspections.

They would come back every two week until the weather turned to cold at which time I brought them inside to do work on the inside of the house and believe me there was a host of work to be done. The kitchen floor which I talked previously was one of the jobs assigned to them and though it wasn't professional they did a credible job and at least we had a kitchen floor now. And with Jewel running her mouth constantly I sought somewhere to go and so I gave Paul and his friend a hundred dollars to clean out the basement and garage. This bothered me that Keith was there but no propensity for work and refused to take the money offered to him and so these young white teens stated it and worked with all the gusto one could ask for and when they were finished they would come to me as manner able as any two kids I'd ever seen. They even did some exterminating getting rid of a rat who had terrorized the house for months and had camped out in the basement. I had no complaints.

A couple of months went by and the weather soon was warm again and those weeds were starting to inflame Jewel once again.

Now I didn't always have the money to pay Paul on the day he would cut the grass or do the work but as soon as I would get it I would give it to he or his parents. I did this without fail. I thought this only fair. If he worked he should be paid. The system had worked well for going on two years until one time I called paid on a Thursday and told him I'd pay him the following day on Friday my pay day. This had never been a problem but today it was and I stared at him incredulously,"Don't I always pay you when I say I'm gonna pay you?"

"Yes you do Mr. Brown but your wife doesn't and she still owes us money." I was shocked and embarrassed. I'd been dealing with these boys for close to two years and had never had a problem and Jewel was always pleased. Well, at least she was as pleased as Jewel could be.

"Jewel I'm out here with Paul trying to get these fella to do the yard and they're refusing saying you owe them money. What's up? Do you owe them?"

She admitted that they'd done work for her and she hadn't paid them.

"Well, do you have their money?"

"No."

I didn't get paid until the following week and for the first time since I'd known him my credit was no good.

"Paul haven't I always paid you?"

"Yes, Mr. Brown but your wife hasn't," he said before turning and walking away.

I felt awful. For years I'd done business where my word was the only thing needed so I always made good on what I said and herewas a seventeen year old kid suddenly telling me my word wasn't good because I now shared it with my wife who was less credible than I. I walked back in the house to find Jewel sitting in her usual Saturday spot in the living room. I stared at her incredulously and wondered how she'd rationalize this one. After all, she was never wrong and never took responsibility for any of her gaffs. As hard as I'd worked to establish some credibility she'd worked just as hard to destroy hers. I stared at her and winced. In Pittsburgh for fifty years and her credibility was awful. Neither her mother nor anyone else would trust her with anything. I wasn't sure if it was her gambling addiction or actions like these that caused this.

"Jewel do you owe Paul money?"

"Yeah. I owe him twenty dollars. What's the big deal?"

"Jewel the boy won't cut the weeds because you owe him money and haven't paid him. Do you have any intentions on paying him?"

139

"I'm not paying him shit. I don't like the work he does and he shows me no respect. He calls you Mr. Brown and he calls me Jewel."

Child Support

After a month or so in Pittsburgh I hired on with a temp
agency and was sent to a moving and storage company.
The job site was a nice little hike and although I had to be
at work at eight o'clock in the morning I had to be up at
four thirty just to be on time. I'd take the bus to the train
and then had to walk a mile or so to the storage company.

In the mornings when I'd leave the house it was still dark
and being that we were newlyweds Jewel would go to the
front window and wave goodbye. I'd cross the street with
my backpack and on more than one occasion there would
be deer or turkeys the size of me blocking my path. Now
these were no ordinary deer like I was accustomed to
seeing in the movies and although they looked like Bambi
they were not to be toyed with. Jewel told me tales of how
they'd head butted Keith so I was more than a little leery.

Not knowing what to do and never having encountered
wild animals of the four legged variety growing up in New
York City I did what any normal person would do in a
similar situation. I said 'shoo shoo' at which time they
looked up at me as if to say this was my home long before
it was yours and refused to move.

I turned back to look at Jewel who appeared to be having a
seizure from laughing. I failed to see the humor. I was

going to miss my bus and lose my job and I certainly couldn't do that with four hungry mouths to feed.

After a few minutes I guess they understood and continued on their way.

The work was hard and didn't pay well but I had no choice. I'd sent out hundreds of resumes and knew that it would take time but I had taken on the responsibility of three growing boys and a wife so I couldn't simply sit back and wait for a good paying job to roll in. No, I had to do something to contribute so I joined in Pittsburgh's version of running with the bulls every morning at the break of dawn.

Most days my days stated at four, four thirty and often I'd work 'til five thirty or six o'clock. So, when I received my first check I was tickled. I raced home and threw it down on the living room table. I was so proud, so happy that I was finally earning; that I could finally contribute to my new family I didn't know what to do.

Jewel picked it up off the table. I knew she would be tickled as well. I looked at her face. Here was three hundred dollars that we didn't have yesterday.

"Well at least we can buy a few groceries."

I was crushed. She didn't appreciate it or the long arduous days I was putting in and once again I questioned myself. Had I made a bad choice?

I didn't like the job but then it had been ingrained in me from a very young age that you weren't going to always like things but some things you just had to grin and bear and once you made a commitment you hed to follow through.

I was no more aware of that than in my first marriage when I was dating a woman that intrigued me and she became pregnant. I loved her but I'm not sure I was ever in live with her. I loved the sex and as a result I had a son and so I did the right thing and married her. I stayed married to her for close to twenty years for the sake of my children. We ended up having a daughter six years after my son was born and I was adamant about not complying with the stereotypical view that Black men were all dead beat dads. More importantly, I had this undying belief that there are more good strong Black fathers and men than are typically portrayed by the media. And this was after years of working as a caseworker for the Bureau of Child Support. I still knew that men like my father and my uncles were in the majority but my arrival in Pittsburgh alas let me know that there is truth in every stereotype.

Jewel was the legal guardian for her two nephews whose father was an addict. I applauded her for taking on this

Heculean task of attempting to raise two children, (although she had no clue of how to raise Black boys).

He own son's father was supposedly this much heralded barber who I was told by her son cuts some of the Pittsburgh Steelers hair. I was hardly impressed not being a Steelers fan and was even less impressed that this man who had fathered this child refused to pay child support. Now it's one thing that he and Jewel had their differences but to not accept responsibilities for your child wasn't something that I could hardly fathom. When she told me that she had taken him to court for child support and the court had only fined him twenty five dollars since he was paid in cash and showed no income to the IRS.

A friend of mine was a barber and another owned a barbershop and I knew that most barbers pay between a hundred and fifty to two hundred dollars a week for a chair. But he refused to pay twenty five dollars a month to support his son. In five years, with Jewel I can honestly say that aside from his birthday and Christmas his son received little or nothing. It was a travesty and being that I saw children and the chance to raise them as a blessing I couldn't understand this.

I can remember taking my son with me when I separated from my first wife and moved to South Carolina. My first couple of months when I moved there it was a transitional period and gave with some perks among those were women

145

and the fact that I lived in an adults only community which gave me access to even more women. All that changed when I went to bring to live with me. No longer was it alright for women to randomly stop by as I didn't want to objectify women in my son's eyes.

When my daughter was born some months later I was shocked when I received papers asking for child support. I already had my son and couldn't understand why my wife would ask for child support for my daughter less than one week after she was born since she was working and had a handsome salary and was quite capable of taking care of my daughter but was so overjoyed by the birth of my daughter that I drove up and grabbed my daughter too. This was no easy task being that I worked three jobs and daycare for my oldest was one job in itself but the opportunity to father my children far outweighed the costs associated with being a father. Financially it meant that I just had to sacrifice some of my own desires and vices.

So, I couldn't even remotely conceive of how this man could possibly consider not feeding his son but this he did while I was doing my best to feed three boys; none of which I had conceived.

I never mentioned this to Jewel but I severely chastised her for her poor choice of men.

"Did you bother to check the resume? What made you lie down with his man and have his child?" I asked her.

"He made me a laugh," she answered.

I couldn't believe her but these days there was a lot I had a hard time believing. I was long convinced that she was no idiot savant by any stretch of the imagination but one of the biggest fools I had ever come to know. And since I was now responsible for their sustenance I asked her to file papers for child support. She had a defeatist attitude when it came to this and was hesitant but finally agreed to. By her reactions I had the feeling that her reenactment of her first marriage and the atrocities that he committed were not his and his alone and now and at this present date and after being with her for years I know that with the lies, coupled with the gambling if he hadn't left I would have questionedhis sanity. On the day she was to appear in court she got up at her usual time and poked around. She was always late but on this date she was later than usual. Having worked for Child Support I knew that court started promptly at nine a.m. and she hadn't even left the house until a quarter after nine. I t all seemed a bit suspicious but I was getting accustomed to the lies and deceit and called a friend of mine who worked in the court system.

"Yes, she was on the docket but she was a no show."

"Are you sure," I asked incredulously. She had to know I was struggling and any financial assistance that we could get to help us with the bills would help immensely. And to ask for a man to be accountable for his son was not too much to ask in my opinion. I didn't know the man and though he didn't want to care for his son's welfare was sinful and wrong in my eyes there was little I could do.

What bothered me though was that she didn't have the empathy to see my plight in all of this. What was even worse was that I had long ago come to the conclusion that Jewel was a pathological liar. I wasn't sure how to approach the situation when she got home from work. As adamant as I was about her going to court I would have to ask her how court had gone. Yet, if she'd said it had gone okay I knew I would lose it. I just didn't want her to lie to me again.

"Hey bay," she said kissing me lightly.

"How was your day?"

"Long."

"How was court?"

"He didn't show."

"Did you?"

Yeah, I was there."

Atlantic City

"Bay! Bay! Do you remember me telling you how Ms. Burnie's club arranges trips?"

"I sorta remember something…"

"That's cause you never listen to anything I say."

She was right in that regard. I had long ago come to the realization that Jewel could and would ramble on about anything and so I long ago learned to turn a deaf ear on a good deal of her idle chatter.

"What about MS.Burnie?"

"Well. You know I told you she's a part of the Ebony Sisters and they arrange bus trips and cruises. Well, they've arranged a bus trip to Atlantic City."

This was not good news and I knew that she was not thinking boardwalks, beaches and sand.

"You wanna go? It'll be fun," Her eyes had that sparkle and that wasn't good.

"When is it?" I asked trying to buy some time and looking for any excuse to get out of it. I didn't gamble so I had a difficult time trying to see how she had come t the conclusion that this trip would be fun for me.

"The end of November. I 'm not sure. I have to check the dates. The money has to be in two weeks. Come on bay. It'll be fun."

There goes Christmas I thought.

"I'm a little short right now."

"So, you'll go. I'll give Ms. Burnie the money on Friday and you can pay me back."

I began to shake. I could feel the sweat bead on the bridge of my nose. Jewel didn't play when it came to money and I knew I'd pay. I just wasn't sure how. The bus and hotel were one thing but that damn casino was a whole different story. I knew as soon as we got there she would no longer see me as her husband but Quicken Loans and I knew I only had a few weeks for something to come up. Nothing did.

On the morning that we left I knew I'd made another terrible mistake.

"Why are you wearing that?"

This was one f the reasons I'd enlisted into the Marines at seventeen. My mother had this same sort of parental authority thing working that I detested so much. But at fifty four I was raise its ugly head again in the form of a wife. I knew then that I was in trouble but committed not to say anything.

The bus ride was like any other six hour bus ride but I was prepared with my laptop, movies and games to play. It had become more or less a nightly tradition that she and I would play Scrabble and so when I asked her to play I thought this would ease some of her anxiety but instead it only served to rile her even more. I guess it wasn't dark enough.

"No, I don't want to play," she said like a petulant two year old turning away from me and putting her butt on my leg.

I wouldn't ask her anything else I said to myself. It then dawned on me that this was the way I used to act when I was trying to score some drugs and they were just beyond my reach. She was fiending to spin the wheel. I tried to console her with conversation.

"You have a hard time riding if you're not driving don't you?"

"Yeah," she acknowledged turning and putting her head on my shoulder. Afraid to move I let her rest it there for the remainder of the trip. Not being able to smoke also was another factor that made her crankier than usual and so I did little to disturb her.

Just prior to arriving Ms. Burney stood and began handing out our room keys and the hundred dollars or so in chips for the casino. I got a hundred and Jewel got a hundred. Hotel employees stepped onto the bus when Ms. Burney had finished and announced they would have everyone's bags in the rooms within in an hour. Jewel was elated and I thought she was going to knock the hotel employee over trying to get off the bus. The chips had to be activated and Jewel snatched mine and hers.

"Whatcha gonna do bay?"

"I'm going up to the room."

I loved hotels. To me hotels meant good times. I was either away in some place other than home, on vacation or it meant sex and with Jewel it often meant both.

"Okay bay", she was happy now and I knew the last thing on her mind was being cooped up in a hotel room with me for any reason. She was here to gamble. That and nothing more... She had three whole days to do nothing more than push buttons and let the machines bleed her dry and she was happy. Food and sleep were something she may have had to do but not if she could help it. I resigned myself to checking out the room and the hotel the first night when she came in to give the room the once over. We'd been to countless hotels together and though the room was quite nice it was especially nice to her because she was close to her favorite venue now. I went down and sat next to her for a few minutes but it soon became apparent that she was in her element and I was distracting her from her favorite pastime and so I made my leave and went to see what the hotel had to offer. Aside from people walking around like drug crazed addicts trying to decide what machine was going to payoff in millions I saw little of interest and headed back to the room. I stopped back where I'd seen her last.

"Jewel why don't you play with your chips and let me have mine so you have something to play with tomorrow?"

"No, bay. I'm not going to use them. I'm tired anyway. Where are you going?"

"Up to the room."

"Okay bay. I'll be up in a few."

Never once did she glance in my direction. I could have been standing there with a woman on each arm and she would have never noticed. She was gone; entrenched in her addiction. To this day she will tell you that she doesn't have a problem but after serving an addiction of my own for years it was easy to recognize. It was even easier to see when she came up to the room later that night.

"How'd you do?"

I'd seen the look before. There was a certain serenity. She lost would have much rather won but she had played and had the chance to win and so she was good almost ecstatic. For her as long as she was competing she had a chance to win.

"I lost."

"Did you spend all your chips?"

"Yeah."

"Did you spend mine too?"

"Yeah."

I turned over and went to sleep. She climbed into the bed, snuggled up to me. She was happy.

The next morning she was up with a lurch.

"Oh my God bay! Do you see what time it is."

Jewel never but never got up on her accord. When it was time to go to work I'd wake her up. She would always check the time before telling me to wake her in another fifteen minutes. But not today. Today she was bright eyed and bushy tailed.

"Come on bay. It's almost nine o'clock. They stop serving breakfast at nine."

I threw on something and headed down to breakfast. After breakfast Jewel headed back to her normal position at the penny machine while I headed back to the room. All out of chips I knew she had a little cash although I had no idea how much.

I lay on the bed and dozed off wondering why I'd come.
Early that evening I awoke to the sound of the door closing.

"Bay it's time for dinner."

The buffet was enormous and I couldn't remember a buffet
being that extravagant or the food being that good. After
dinner Jewel returned with me to the room which was not a
good sign.

"Bay can I have some money?"

I'd bought a little more than hundred or so just in case of
emergency and here it was. She was out of money with
almost two days to go and I knew this was the beginning of
the end.

A couple of hours later she was back.

"Bay do you have any money?"

"I gave you my last Jewel. I took my last twenty and
bought cigarettes," I said holding up three packs. I usually
bought her cigarettes when I bought my own but she I'd
given her all my money except for twenty dollars and just
naturally assumed she'd buy some.

"Well, call your son and ask him to wire you some money."

I looked at her like she was crazy.

"You want me to call my twenty five year old son and ask him to wire me money so you can gamble," I said hoping she could hear herself.

"I'll pay him back."

"Then you call him."

"I'm not calling him. Look at yourself."

The fact is an addict cannot and does not have the ability to look at or hear themselves.

"Then call your sister."

"Are you crazy? Listen Jewel. You spent what they gave you to spend. Then you spent mine. You spent your money and then you spent mine and now you're asking me to call my family and have them wire you some more money so you can throw that away too. No. I'm not going to do it."

"Well, call your fat ass friend. She'll do anything for you."

I wanted to ask her why she didn't call her own family and her own mother but I already knew the answer to that and so did she but that wasn't the end of it.

After sitting there staring at me for what seemed forever she grabbed her bag and walked out slamming the door behind her.

I couldn't believe her. What was supposed to be a relaxing few days was turning out to be a nightmare. The whole time we'd been married we had never been financially stable and I would honestly say that her gambling contributed to us never being able to put anything away or us never having anything for a rainy day. We lived payday to payday with us barely making it from one to the next. Now here she was trying to borrow so that we could be in even more debt when we returned home. But I wouldn't be scuffling and apologizing to my family when she refused to pay.

I didn't see Jewel anymore that day and when dinner time came around I began to wonder where she was. We always met for dinner and it was getting late so I searched the casino and hotel after sitting on the boardwalk for a while. I tried to call but she wasn't picking up. Dinner was about to be over and since I hadn't heard from her I walked to the restaurant and questioned why I'd come. I could have saved two hundred dollars and stayed home and watched television alone.

On the way in I saw her coming out and called my wife who looked at me and kept walking without speaking. I called her again and she continued without speaking.

Epitaph

The sad affairs that I describe in this book are believe it or not true and did occur during my six year marriage. At times I attempted to put a humorous tint to many of the events that occurred. At other times I simply wrote things as they actually occurred as many of the events were too painful for me to poke fun at.

Recollecting I believe that a marriage or a union between two people is voluntary and is only as strong as the bond of trust between them. This union cannot grow and strengthen if it is built on lies and deceit which our marriage was.

I am and was however a contributor to its collapse and take a good deal of responsibility for its demise. However, much of my frustration came from the fact that this woman who I continue to love dearly has never taken responsibility for any of her lies or deceit.

She filed for divorce this past week and then emailed me to ask if she could still attend my family reunion with me. She then called to tell me that the next time I was going to do the right thing and buy her a ring before we got married again. Read the book. Tell me what the possibilities of that are.

CPSIA information can be obtained at www.ICGtesting.com
Printed in the USA
LVOW01s2013090714

393589LV00023B/1340/P